# SPECTRUMS

*of related interest*

**Trans and Autistic**
Stories from Life at the Intersection
*Noah Adams and Bridget Liang*
ISBN 978 1 78592 484 2
eISBN 978 1 78450 875 3

**Supporting Transgender Autistic Youth and Adults**
A Guide for Professionals and Families
*Finn V. Gratton, LMFT, LPCC*
*Illustrated by Harper Cheaney*
ISBN 978 1 78592 803 1
eISBN 978 1 78450 830 2

**Uncomfortable Labels**
My Life as a Gay Autistic Trans Woman
*Laura Kate Dale*
ISBN 978 1 78592 587 0
eISBN 978 1 78592 588 7

**Gender Identity, Sexuality and Autism**
Voices from Across the Spectrum
*Eva A. Mendes and Meredith R. Maroney*
*Foreword by Wenn Lawson*
ISBN 978 1 78592 754 6
eISBN 978 1 78450 585 1

**Transitioning Together**
One Couple's Journey of Gender and Identity Discovery
*Wenn B. Lawson and Beatrice M. Lawson*
ISBN 978 1 78592 103 2
eISBN 978 1 78450 365 9

# SPECTRUMS

*Autistic Transgender People
in Their Own Words*

**Edited by Maxfield Sparrow**

**Jessica Kingsley Publishers**
London and Philadelphia

First published in 2020
by Jessica Kingsley Publishers
73 Collier Street
London N1 9BE, UK

*www.jkp.com*

Copyright © Jessica Kingsley Publishers 2020

Front cover image source: Waewkidja, Freepik.

**Library of Congress Cataloging in Publication Data**
A CIP catalog record for this book is available from the Library of Congress

**British Library Cataloguing in Publication Data**
A CIP catalogue record for this book is available from the British Library

ISBN 978 1 78775 014 2
eISBN 978 1 78775 015 9

Printed and bound in Great Britain

To every person on the spectrum who has paused to think about gender and every Trans, non-binary, and gender-nonconforming person who learned of Autistic traits and mused, "I'm just like that."
Your search for your deepest and truest self is beautiful to behold.

# Acknowledgments

I am deeply grateful for my editors at Jessica Kingsley Publishers: Andrew James and Sean Townsend. My editors had the patience of saints, the blue pencils of angels, and offered the support and compassion only seen from the highest caliber of human beings. All errors are my own; all editing genius solely theirs. Thank you.

Dear ones, in no particular order, who kept me alive and writing: Fermat the Wonder Cat (aka Mister Kitty), Jane Lose, Andrew Dell'Antonio, Fred Alger, Ash Ford, Ana Maria Young, Morgan Peterson, Natalie Earnhart, Kelsey Rellas, London Earnhart, Jessie Glasscock and the Usual Suspects at BPM, A Girl Named Earl, Jeff Newman, Christine, Sammy Moore, Sam Cook, Chris Chady, Stephanie Hempel, Elijah Nixon, Arthur Hull and the Boulder/Longmont/Loveland drumming community, Joelle Maslak, Leslie Rice, Hanya Alger, J'Lyn Chapman, Serena Chopra, Caroline "Swanee" Swanson, Jeffrey Pethybridge.

Finally, there are two people without whom I wouldn't even exist: Carolyn and Wayne Jones. Thank you, Mommy and Daddy, for the gift of life and every priceless gift since.

# Contents

# Introduction

*Maxfield Sparrow (they/them/their)*

In the early aughts, I was writing about gender and presenting my papers at conferences. For one gender conference, I decided I wanted to research and write about the intersection of autism and gender, two topics so close to my heart it was as much "me-search" as research. Eagerly, I approached the academic databases and started typing search terms. A few hours later, I turned off my computer, so disheartened I went into a depression. I didn't write anything about autism and gender and I didn't even attend that conference.

What I had unearthed was the earliest research about Transgender[1] Autists. Or Autistic Transgender folks—whichever way you want to spin that phrase. For me, there's only a subtle difference between the two because both identities are so woven into my core being that "person with autism" sounds just as detached and jarring to me as "person with transgenderism." (In fact, there are many people in the Trans community (and I'm one of them) who cringe at the word "transgenderism" because it has historically been used so often by people who want to objectify, pathologize, and demean those who experience genders that do not match the gender we were assigned at birth,[2] presenting us as diseased and dangerous.)

To put this identity disconnect in perspective for those who identify with a binary gender, imagine describing someone as a "person with femaleness" or a "person with maleness." It probably sounds odd and unnecessary to you, using language to separate someone's gender from their core identity and personhood that way. That's how tightly woven in my identities as an Autist and a Trans person are. Not all people on the autism spectrum feel that way and not all gender variant and gender-nonconforming people feel that way, either. But for so many of us, these identities are deeply rooted in our being.

What did I find in my literature search back in those earliest years of the 21st century? There wasn't much research out there and what little I found were individual case studies. We were many years yet from the research that is currently re-tooling the way people see autism: the studies that show that Autists assigned female at birth often have more skill at masking or camouflaging the signs of their autism—whether due to some inherent biological trait or as a result of the differences in how those children viewed as female are socialized and the different set of expectations laid on them due to presumptions about their gender role. We were still deeply in "one in four" territory[3] with respect to autism and gender back then. And we were even further from the prevalence studies examining groups of people living in the intersection of autism and gender identity.

Those few case studies 20 years ago were of Autistic children who had firmly declared their gender—a gender that didn't match the one that had been assigned to them at birth. The papers were deeply pathologizing, casting these children as engaged in an autistic obsession with gender, not as the Transgender children I could so clearly see them as. The children's frustration with the adults around them was so palpable it leaked through the detached scientific language of the white coats writing about them.

Don't get me wrong, I love researchers. They are our lifelines from a different, better future. We Autists and we Trans folks can tell the world who we are for generations without seeing any change. But when researchers hear us and study the things we are telling them, the results are life-transforming. More and more researchers are including us in their work, listening to us, and studying us as fellow human beings who deserve a place at society's table. I can see the positive impact their work is having on all our Autistic lives, ranging from increased access to communication to more diverse job and career opportunities and everything in between.

So I don't sneer at autism researchers, but those researchers I was reading that long-ago day were not our allies. They were not listening to their patients, but viewing them through a medicalizing lens that left no room for the possibility that an Autist might have enough empathy, theory of mind, and cognitive capacity to actually be transgender, recognize themselves as such, and clearly communicate that understanding to others. The children in those early case studies were not being treated as whole human beings with autonomy and self-understanding. It was beyond upsetting.

The landscape is different today. There are still medical journal articles, published within the last five years, that describe our gender experiences in terms of autistic deficits. I'm still reading interpretations of our words and actions that feel like they are coming more from a researcher's lens than an Autist's experiences. But the overall view I got when I recently combed through scores of journal articles was much more positive than the scientific landscape of two decades ago. I came away from journal reading this time filled with hope, not despair.

I couldn't help contrasting the pain I felt at reading those early case studies with the joy I felt reading a case study published in 2018[4] describing an extremely anxious child who had been diagnosed with autism at age two. At age eight, the child was minimally speaking, mostly using an iPad to communicate. The child's parents brought him to a gender clinic because he became upset when people referred to him as "she," insisting "Don't say she! Say HE!" An autism-informed gender therapist worked with the child and his family, helping to facilitate a transition to recognizing the child as a boy. The results were astounding:

The child made no eye contact, shied from any physical contact, and anxiously hummed and rocked. After several months of mental health treatment...[t]he clinic team was astounded to discover a child who strode into the clinic, shook hands with the team, made eye contact, and began talking in full, although truncated, sentences. (p.4080)

So much of what had led diagnosticians to label the child as "severely autistic" turned out to be layers of anxiety and gender dysphoria. This case sheds so much light on both the intersection of autism and transgender issues and the true nature of what we tend to label as being an inherent part of autism. How many of the struggles of autism would dissolve in a world where Autists were accepted, accommodated, and valued for who we are rather than who we might be shaped into?

## PREVALENCE AT THE INTERSECTION

It was the prevalence studies that convinced me this anthology was sorely needed. Autistic people have a higher rate of Transgender identities than the general population does. Likewise, the Transgender community has a higher autism rate than the general population. Before getting into the (widely varying) numbers found in prevalence studies, what are the general rates of autism and Trans people?

The US Centers for Disease Control and Prevention (CDC) report a worldwide autism prevalence rate between 1 and 2 percent of the population.[5] The UK's National Autistic Society (NAS) reports a similar rate, between 1 and 2 percent; about 700,000 people in the UK are Autistic.[6]

Finding a prevalence rate for Trans people is more difficult. Many Trans people don't want to be counted. Many don't identify as transgender (some of those people are non-binary[7] and don't identify as cisgender[8] or transgender. Some have binary[9] genders and identify as, for example, "a man with a trans history"). The definition of transgender (e.g. only counting people who medically transition, only counting people reporting gender dysphoria, only counting trans people with binary gender identities) can vary from one prevalence study to another, dramatically affecting reported prevalence rates.

The most recent edition of the *Diagnostic and Statistical Manual of Mental Disorders (DSM-5)* cites a prevalence range between 0.002 percent and 0.014 percent[10] with lower numbers for Trans people assigned female at birth than those assigned male at birth, but warns that it's only counting referrals to gender clinics so the numbers are artificially low. Numbers from other sources for binary, medically transitioning transgender people range from 0.004 percent to 0.027 percent.[11] (While both these numbers come from a single New Zealand study, they are, coincidentally, the far ends of range estimates from a number of studies from the US, Netherlands, and UK.)

Prevalence rates for trans people go up dramatically when looking at the larger population, not just those who show up at clinics to medically transition or those who change their gender on their passport and other vital documents. A 2016 review and meta-analysis[12] including prevalence studies that relied on self-reporting of trans status found prevalence rates in a range from 0.1 percent (from the California Health Interview Survey) to 7.3 percent (from a Taiwanese survey of first-year college students). The significant size of the prevalence range from self-reported transgender studies illustrates the difficulty in assessing just how many trans people there might be among the general population.

With this general (and sometimes frustratingly vague) understanding of the individual prevalence rates of Autists and Trans people, let's turn to the rates of intersection between these two identities. It's much easier to see that Trans people have higher rates of autism than vice versa, due to the inconsistencies surrounding gender studies and definitions guiding research into trans populations.

I reviewed many intersectional prevalence studies and found that transgender people range from demonstrating no significant difference in autistic traits/diagnosis when compared to cisgender people[13] to Trans people testing in an autistic range at a 23.1 percent rate,[14] over ten times the rate found in the general population. Studies between those two extremes found autism rates of 2.2 percent,[15] 3 percent,[16] 4.8 percent,[17] 5.5 percent,[18] 6.3 percent,[19] 7.8 percent,[20] 11 percent,[21] and 14.5 percent[22] among transgender populations—all above the 1–2 percent found in the general population.

With a wider variation of reported rates of Transgender, non-binary, and gender variant people among the general population, I leave it to the reader to decide if Autistic people have elevated rates of gender variance when studies report rates of 0.07 percent,[23] 1.9 percent,[24] 3.8 percent,[25] 3.9 percent,[26] 5.4 percent,[27] 7.2 percent,[28] 8 percent,[29] 11.3 percent,[30] or 22 percent.[31]

## THE NEED FOR THIS ANTHOLOGY

The data may be confusing, but one thing was clear to me: the world needs to hear more from the people who actually live at the intersection of autism and gender variance. Research is important, but nothing can replace the wisdom and knowing that comes from lived experience.

Being Autistic and being Transgender, non-binary, or otherwise gender divergent have much in common, both joys and struggles. The joys come from deep self-knowledge, belonging to a community, living a life in tune with one's inner being. A few struggles in common include suicide, homelessness, and barriers to adequate healthcare.

*The Lancet* reported in 2017 that two-thirds of Autistic adults have experienced suicidal thoughts and 35 percent have planned or attempted suicide.[32] Studies reported in a 2013 paper found suicide attempt rates of 41 percent and 43 percent among Transgender people.[33] No one has studied whether belonging to two groups with high suicide risks creates an additive (or multiplicative, or exponential) risk for an individual.

Studies in the UK found that 12 percent of Autistic people were homeless and 65 percent of homeless sleeping in the streets were Autistic.[34] In the US, the National Center for Transgender Equality estimates that one in five Transgender people have experienced homelessness at some point in their life.[35] Again, I know of no studies that have looked at the effects of living with multiple marginalizations known to lead to poverty and homelessness.

Autistic people have higher rates of many healthcare issues, ranging from seizure disorders to allergies and autoimmune disorders, as well as higher rates of mental health issues including, but not limited to, depression and anxiety. Communication issues and economic pressures, among other barriers, limit Autistic access to adequate healthcare.[36] Transgender and other gender variant people have similar healthcare access issues, with a different (but overlapping) set of causes, including economic barriers, discrimination, and lack of provider education.[37]

The authors collected in this anthology address the struggles and joys of living at the intersection of neurodivergence and gender divergence with personal insight and nuance rarely, if ever, found in academic studies. Herein you will find human stories: lives filled with pain and pleasure, accomplishments and setbacks. The flesh-and-blood realities of the contributors' lives will teach you more than you can get from any list of statistics or citations of research studies.

We're pleased to offer you glimpses into our lives, thoughts, and experiences. Welcome, and we hope you enjoy the journey.

Trigger warning: This book mentions suicide as well as drugs/substance use.

# My Body

*Joelle Smith (she/her/hers)*

I want to write to my siblings—sisters, brothers, and siblings-of-genders-beyond-number. I want to talk about expressions of power in a world that so often exerts power over us. I particularly want to write to those of you considering whether you should take the incredible leap to being yourself—of transitioning.

I won't pretend this is easy. The path ahead of us is hard, but so was the path behind us.

One of my earliest memories is an attempt at suicide. I don't remember how old I was, but I think it was around age seven. What I most remember is the despair. I did what some people who want to die do—try to kill myself. In my case, I wrapped a chain around my neck tightly and allowed my body weight to pull me down. I waited for death to find me, the chain supporting my tiny frame's weight.

I don't remember exactly why I felt this despair, but I'm glad I failed at that and other attempts. I do know that I was treated horribly at school, a hell I am astonished I survived, as at the time I felt very small and very weak. Today, I can look in the mirror and (at least sometimes) see a proud, strong woman looking back at me. That's a view I never thought I'd see. I certainly couldn't have predicted I'd see this view when I was a small child, nor even as a teenager. And I hope anyone who reads this finds whatever they need to find to avoid that fate. It's why I wanted to write this—to speak to the hope that remains even when it is dark outside. As Miss Major famously said,

"I want my trans girls and guys to stand up and say, 'I'm still fucking here!'" But I'm getting ahead of myself. I was desperate to have control over something as a kid.

Back then, as a child, I didn't know why I didn't fit in the world. While home was a safe place, the rest of world was not, and that world made it clear that it had no place for me. This was a lie, but it was a lie repeated often. If I were to forget, I had constant reminders of this lie. I was desperate to try to fit into the square hole the world told me to fit into, but an autistic trans girl just cannot force herself through a square hole, no matter how hard she tries.

In those early grades, I was the "boy" who broke the unwritten rules. One of my earliest memories was being told to stop playing with one set of kindergarten toys (building blocks) during play time and instead to play with some other toy. Preferring the same toy every day just wouldn't do in the eyes of the teachers. Doing the same thing every day is reserved for your dull, repetitive adult job, and is wholly unsuitable for kindergartners! So, I was forced to alternate days where I played with blocks with days where I played with other toys. Unfortunately, I chose the one thing that was apparently worse than playing with blocks on those alternate days: I joined the girls to play with the dolls. Despite what the teachers said about just wanting me to play with something else, I received an early lesson in unwritten rules. There are boys' toys and there are girls' toys, and the categories should never mix! That lesson took a while for me to understand, but through repeated incidents like this one, I eventually learned it. It's a lesson I wish nobody was forced to learn.

At the time, I didn't know I was autistic, and that's why I liked to play with the same toy every day. I didn't know that I have a mind that excels at creating things, of building ordered systems from a collection of simple parts, a skill that is somewhat common among autistic people. It's also a skill that has enabled me to succeed professionally, and it was a skill that, fortunately, was not any easier for teachers to kill off than it was for me to take my own life. I think I have my autistic perseveration to thank for that.

I also didn't know I was a girl. If you asked me, I would have said I was a boy, because nobody told me that all these adults around me might have got it wrong. All I knew was that I liked doing the things the girls did. I liked hanging out with the girls. I enjoyed making up stories while playing with the dolls, in that cooperative kind of play where everyone can win. But that's not what boys were supposed to do! Just as you can't erase someone's autism without erasing the entirety of their life, you can't erase someone's femininity, even if they were born into a body that doesn't look like the bodies of the other girls.

I can relate many other stories, although as I look back through those stories, I can see how a small autistic girl tried to be who she was created to be despite attempts to force her through that square hole. I can see who her precious few friends were, what games she played at recess, what her interests were, what books she read, and what TV shows she watched. Through these, I can see how that small autistic girl was always there, even before I knew she was. I can see how, too often, she was punished for that, and how she was left trying to find ways of having some say in her own life, of owning her life and body. I needed to own something. I suspect that's what that early suicide attempt was about, in some small way. Destroying the body wouldn't have given me ownership, though, so I'm glad I found other ways.

For instance, a few years later I contracted chicken pox (the vaccine was not routinely given to children then). It gave me an unexpected chance to own my body a little bit. I remember it being a few weeks of misery, under quarantine, and being told not to itch the incredibly itchy welts over every part of my body. I was told, "If you itch or pick at these spots, you'll get a scar." So, I tried not to itch them. But when one appeared on the center of my forehead, I did pick at it—and sure enough I now have a scar there. It was my way of marking myself, to express my femininity. It was purposeful and intentional, but not in the way someone else would recognize. That made it safe. Secrets were safe, even when they were literally in plain sight on my face.

Why picking at a scab? How is that feminine? Long before I heard the term "cultural appropriation," I had seen on TV some Asian women, particularly Indian, with dots on their foreheads—something I felt accentuated their beauty (and which I've learned since is rich and nuanced in cultural meaning beyond superficial beauty, something I sadly didn't appreciate at that young age). So, when I had the chance to mark my forehead, I did. I wanted some of that same beauty. When you're often suicidal (which I was at this point still), having some way of expressing who you are can save your life, even if that expression will be lost on everyone around you. While I don't think I'd make this same choice today (out of respect for other cultures), I look at it as the first of many changes I've made to my body to mold it into something that fits me better. When I look at myself in the mirror, I still see this scar, and will never make an effort to hide it. It's a mark of survival.

There were a few more scars I acquired during childhood—proof that this woman is made of tough stuff. Some were the results of what other people did to me. I have faded scars on one arm of burns I received from other kids for being a "fag" (incidentally this is why I know reparative therapy is useless—I had plenty of motivation to become straight). I have a scar on my hip that is accompanied by vivid memories of rocks being picked out of it in the emergency room (I got that one from flying down a hill way too fast on a bicycle). But I have a scar on the right arm that is still a mystery. It's a three-inch-long, nearly perfectly straight line. Like the other scars, it's proof of my survival even if the origin is unknown. I'll get back to this.

For the next couple decades, I hid my secret, but how I wished I could express who I was with the clothing, hair, and makeup I wanted to wear. How I wished I could be one of the girls, and how I wished I could quit being one of the guys. Eventually I realized that hiding this part of me was killing me. Sure, it was doing so a lot slower than my childhood suicide attempts would have, but there was no future for me if I didn't do something.

So after decades of hiding this, I decided to live. But let's get back to the scar.

It's that scar on my arm that was powerful confirmation that I now live, that I now own my body. Fast-forwarding many years, to adulthood, I finally could understand there was a reason I wished I was a girl, a reason why I could relate to women, and why masculinity never seemed like a good fit for me. When I finally had the courage to begin transition, one of the first things I did was to remove the body hair that covered my arms and legs. While I had fairly thick hair, it wasn't thick enough to hide my skin. Even so, I remember my shock when I saw this scar on my arm. Where did that come from? Why hadn't I noticed it?

I've asked my family about it—they don't remember the origin of this scar either, which is surprising. I have a hard time understanding how I could have such a scar with no memory of it. My doctor thinks it may be a scar from a muscle biopsy, but my childhood records are long gone. Being that my upper body has always been disproportionately weak—an unsolved medical puzzle from childhood—that's certainly possible. Whatever it was, it was from long enough ago that it's not in my medical records anymore, and the cause doesn't really matter. The relevant aspect of the scar is that I somehow went decades (I assume) with it on my arm without ever noticing. That's what happens when your body doesn't fit: you don't notice a three-inch-long scar! While I'm no expert on how we relate to our bodies, I'm sure I didn't relate to mine. Save for that scar on my forehead, it wasn't really my body. It was just the body I occupied. I was disinterested in my body. I was disinterested enough that I don't remember it getting injured in this way, nor remember seeing it in the thousands of showers I've taken.

Shaving that hair changed everything. Body hair is what most triggers my dysphoria. Shaving it, watching it circle and empty down the shower drain, was powerful. When I looked at myself in the mirror, I cried. Not the tears of despair, but the tears of hope and joy. I saw me, for the first time ever. I had claimed ownership over this bag of mostly water I occupied. This body wasn't a useless sack of fluid, now it was my body. Certainly, I wish the rest of the dysphoria was as easy to wash away as the body hair was, but I can say that a razor gave me a life.

I've taken many steps since then to take ownership of my body. It's my body now. I want it to reflect the soul it houses, so I continue to personalize it to match who I am. I have fond memories of paying someone to jab a needle through my ear lobes (I love dangly earrings, so stimmy!). Having this ownership is what gave me permission to medically shift my body's hormonal balance from male to female, a change that made my emotions my own in the same way that shaving my body hair made my arm my own. There are other steps I've taken, and some I will take in the future, and every one of these steps seems to bring confirmations that my body is mine and that I am part of this world.

Sometimes people ask if I've had regrets since transitioning. The answer is simple: hell no! I now have a body that is my own. I am increasingly seen as I am, not as someone I'm pretending to be. I've had more joy in the last couple years of life than I had in the nearly four decades before them. I am a woman! How could I possibly regret any of that? No, I'm not regretful. I'm thankful.

I do have regrets I waited so long to do this. I was scared. This is a scary thing to do. While I couldn't have transitioned as a child, I wish I transitioned when I first learned the label for the kind of person I am. But there is another part of me that looks at the scars, not just the physical ones that I can see in the mirror. That part of me looks at the invisible scars and knows that she is a strong person. No, not just a strong person, she is a strong woman! I sometimes think it would have been so much easier if I managed to transition when I was young, not four decades into life. But I also don't think I'd be the person I am today if I had.

I've had a similar experience learning of my autism and learning to embrace it. It's not a bad thing to be focused on something so much you want to experience everything that you can about it. I'm that way with computers. I find great joy in doing something with computers every day, even if my kindergarten teachers would be horrified to learn that I play with the same "toy" every day! I've learned to embrace my sensory difference, my social differences, and my personality differences. I'm exactly who I was created to be.

I don't know you, the reader, and I can't tell you what to do in your unique situation. But I do know a few things. If you're feeling weak or hopeless, I want you to know that I know you're strong. Even without knowing you, I know you are strong because your life has had struggles and trouble. You might be going through pure hell right now. I wish I could fix that for you. I wish I could fix the world that destroys too many strong, amazing, and unique souls. I can't do that. But I hope you press on and do what you have to do to see tomorrow. And then when the opportunity to own your body appears, whether it's a safe secret thing only you will know, or whether it is the decision to say, "Fuck it!" and to live as yourself in all aspects of your life, I'm rooting for you. I always bet on the trans person winning this battle because trans people are fucking awesome. And despite what the odds-makers might say, betting on trans people is no long-shot bet.

I'm thankful that I failed at those early attempts to kill myself, those attempts from before I knew the words for who I am, before I knew I was trans, before I knew I was autistic. I'm glad I got to see the strong woman that I am in the mirror. I hope you get to see yourself in your mirror.

But what matters most is that I'm still fucking here. I'm glad you are too.

*Joelle has been writing about her autism for over 20 years. She recently started living her authentic life as a woman and loves to share that joy with others.*

# I'm Just Me

*Ben James (he/him/his)*

I used to think, "I'm just weird, I just don't belong anywhere," before I realized who I was.

Discovering I was both autistic and trans was an adventure for me. At roughly 16 or 17 years old, I was talking to my mother in a shop and told her about a friend of mine being diagnosed as autistic, and she quickly told me, "You're autistic too, you know." I had no idea until this point, but it suddenly made so many things make sense to me; why I was the way I was as a child, why I struggled so much to fit in with others, why I had such intense interests that others couldn't seem to relate to. It was like a wake-up call, and it let me understand why I felt the need to rock, why I couldn't understand the people around me, why I couldn't understand when they did things they didn't like or said things they didn't mean. I felt like I understood myself so much more. Shortly after that, I started figuring out that female pronouns just felt wrong for some reason. I had my friends change pronouns to masculine ones, and then after even longer I decided on changing my name. I decided to make my name Ben, as it was the name of a character in one of my old special interests, and it just felt right to me. Accepting myself as trans and autistic has been difficult—to many people my identities are contradictory. The trans community sometimes dismiss my autism, and claim that I can't be trans because I'm autistic. It took me from 16 until I was 18 to fully embrace my trans identity, and it took me until I was 19 to be able to accept my own autism. Since accepting myself, I have taken part in research on transmasculine individuals, including an interview where I talked about what it's like being both trans and autistic at the same time. I felt so proud being able to be a voice for trans autistic people; being asked how to make the resources available for trans people more accessible to autistic people was a question I had never expected to be asked in my life. I've created an account centered around my autism and standing up for our rights as autistic people and trying to educate people about what life is like as an autistic individual—and through that I have gained so much pride in who I am and have been able to talk to so many other autistic individuals who have wonderful stories to tell.

The way I interact with the world is different. I refuse to do things I don't enjoy because I can't see the point in that. My development is behind everyone else my age, and it has taken me longer than others to learn how to do things, or to be prepared for huge changes, but that's not something I need to be ashamed of. Everyone moves at their own pace. Within the next few years, I plan on becoming independent and leaving my carer. It's something that is scary to think about, but it's something that feels necessary for me to be able to grow more. I also plan to start physically transitioning soon; I'm already transitioning socially right now through coming out to people, and requesting that people refer to me by my chosen name. As a trans autistic person, I feel as if people overall just don't take me seriously. I feel as if my gender isn't taken seriously, nor am I overall, because of the stereotypical vision people have when they think of autistic people. I tried so hard to fit into a very stereotypical idea of what a trans man should be, and I was just never happy that way. I followed people's advice, which said I should get square glasses and never shave my head if I wanted to pass at all. After a while I just decided to ignore that advice and be myself. I've changed my glasses to a rounder shape and I prefer them, I dyed my hair bright pink at one point, I shaved my head one day when I just felt like it, I buy myself cute shirts that fit my kind of style. Caring less about fitting an ideal and caring more about what I am happy doing has made me so much happier, and somehow, I've ended up passing better through just being myself.

I don't fit the stereotypical idea for either a trans or an autistic person but I'm fine with that. I'm just me, this is who I am. I am a trans man who loves cute things, who loves designing clothes, who wants to make his own clothes one day. I'm an autistic person with a deep love for telling stories and communicating with people, even if that's a struggle sometimes. The people I surround myself with fully embrace both parts of my identity and have put in the time and effort to learn about them when they've been unsure.

Instead of thinking I'm weird now, I know that I'm just me, and I'm learning to love that. Gender identity and neurodivergence included.

---

*Ben is a 20-year-old trans man from North East England who dreams of creating comics and graphic novels to share his stories with people.*

# Lifting the Burden

*Drake Keeper (they/them/theirs)*

The experience for me of growing up non-binary, trans, and autistic was a lonely one. The feeling I constantly had and often still have was one of being on the outside, looking in, everywhere I went. When kids are young, categories are perhaps even more important than they are to adults, and gender is among the most important of them all. I didn't fit.

When lunch came, I often sat at the table for those who didn't fit in, or simply didn't get in line quickly enough to get a good seat next to the other boys or girls. A non-verbal autistic kid also sat there on the very end of the table, and I understood that kid in a way that his caretakers could not. We had similar sensitivities, and I could usually tell when he was getting irritated and about to have a meltdown because I was also being overstimulated.

I did not yet know that autism was a spectrum, and that I could be on it. I did not know why we shared similar experiences. I would get overwhelmed by overlapping conversations at high volume or even just the very bright lights at school, or the electrical humming certain rooms have. Nobody knew why I would just start crying inconsolably or lashing out when I was at home. I couldn't tell them, because I didn't understand.

When I first hit puberty, I remember feeling very trapped. I knew that girls grew into women, but I had it in my mind that somehow my growth would be different. Perhaps I would be accepted into

Hogwarts and keep a large supply of polyjuice potions and be able to change into a woman or a man at will. Maybe I would be like those frogs I read about who could change sex. I knew that trans people existed, but I didn't want anyone to get the impression I wanted to be a boy, and I didn't know that there were any other options besides the two genders I had been taught to recognize. I wish that I had known that hormone blockers were even an option for me before I started puberty.

I went my entire childhood without being diagnosed with autism. I also did not come out as trans in that time. I identified as a lesbian. When I experienced dysphoria about my body, I merely pushed it down and hoped it would go away. I avoided looking at mirrors. I thought it was about my body weight at the time. Maybe that was part of it, but it was certainly not the whole of it.

It wasn't until my first year of college that I started asking questions about gender and the possibility that I was autistic. I was home-schooled starting in sixth grade, and I spent most of that time avoiding social contact whenever possible. I had trouble adjusting to regularly spending time in a place with so many people. I was afraid to go into the cafeteria because there were an intimidating number of people there. I had difficulty socially, causing a massive amount of anxiety. I self-medicated with combinations of prescription drugs that seemed to help me relax. I realized that the things that were so difficult for me were intuitive for other people, so I began to research autism.

At the same time, I took an Introduction to Cultural Anthropology class. In that class, there was an entire lecture devoted to anthropology of gender, and it was then that I learned that in anthropology, it was considered fact that there were more than two genders, although gender itself was considered to be socially constructed. I learned about cultures across time and across the world that recognized more than two genders, and I didn't know why that spoke to me.

When I was 19, I dated a trans woman who was a good eight or nine years older than me, and when she described her experiences growing up trans to me, I realized this also resonated with me. I began to question my gender, but when I spoke to my mother about it, she felt that it was because I was easily suggestible and was over-identifying with the woman I was seeing at the time. After that, I spent many years keeping my questioning to myself.

In my mid-20s, I was diagnosed as being on the autism spectrum. Shortly after, I came out to my family as non-binary. I'm not sure exactly when I knew that was who I was, only that at some point, I found a label that felt "right" to me. I asked them to use they/them pronouns for me, which they still struggle with, but at least they are trying.

I realized at some point that I had been carrying a burden of shame and self-loathing my entire life. At the time that I am writing this, I have exactly one week until I have a consultation to go on testosterone. My family do not want me to do this, because they are afraid it will affect my mood and that I will have more meltdowns at home. I've given myself permission to do this for me anyway. I am allowing myself to be free to become the person I am meant to be. Perhaps this is the best gift I have ever given myself.

---

*Drake is an aspiring screenwriter from Birmingham, Alabama. They enjoy spending time with their cat and avoiding human contact.*

# The Queer Phoenix

*Maxx Crow (he/him/his or they/them/their)*

I once heard of a bird, heard its fiery songs,
That bird is beautiful, with intense shades that have no words
Queer would be the word to describe the phoenix.
I said that because that creature is me,
I feel the element inside of me all day,
I feel the need of reincarnation.
I need fire,
Fire to light the herbs I smoke,
Fire to calm my nerves and feel awoke,
To imagine the destruction of hatred
To be reborn as anew, as an avian deity,
As the bird, the phoenix to the mind's eye
I am afraid though, that it burns, that it hurts,
The very soul that has weaken, yet strengthen,
My mind, my mentality that was meant to be broken
This is why I want to be burned alive,
To be one again, to be better than before,
It is said that the phoenix is reborn after 1400 years.
I need fire,
To light myself, to feel the fury,
To indulge in pains and pleasures of the heat.
What else can I do then just burn, and burn,

All day, every day, until the sun burns out its flames,
For the greater good.

---

*Maxx is an anarchist autpunk from California. He enjoys reading and going to punk shows. He's also a non-binary trans guy who is on the spectrum.*

# Bodies with Purpose

### An Exploration of the Intersection of Autistic and Transgender Coding in *Star Trek*

Gil Goletski (they/them/theirs)

Like most modern science fiction, *Star Trek*, although set in the future and on the frontiers of strange alien worlds, is always based in human story. The distance of speculative future to the viewer allows shows like *Star Trek* to explore stories, ethical dilemmas, and lifestyles that would normally be taboo subjects when set in the present. *Star Trek* primarily functions as a study of fictional rhetorical listening. This is a term coined by Krista Ratcliffe,[38] which she defines as a "code of cross-cultural contact...[a] rhetorical stance of openness that a person may choose to assume in cross-cultural exchanges," with the goal being "to generate discourses, whether they be in academic journals or over the dinner table." *Star Trek* invites the viewer into a science fiction, future world in which boundless alien cultures exist; it invites us to empathize, scrutinize, root for, and reject the different characters by generating different discourses within an episodic, serialized structure. *Star Trek* is the dinner table the audience is invited to sit at.

*Star Trek's* utopian view of the future communicates a moral of universal acceptance of difference. *Star Trek* (ideally) promotes empathy. However, Paul Heilker and Melanie Yergeau[39] in "Autism as a rhetoric," interrogate empathy itself, employing Ratcliffe's rhetorical listening; in order to listen properly, we must rethink how we have been taught to listen. *Star Trek: The Next Generation* and *Star Trek: Deep Space Nine* bring empathy into crisis through characters like Data, Jadzia Dax, and Odo. Through explorations of their personalities and (multiple) lives, the viewers become familiar with their inherent neurological queerness (a term coined by Melanie Yergeau[40] in her book *Authoring Autism: On Rhetoric and Neurological Queerness*). Neurological queerness denotes observing cognitive difference from a queer theory stance; to accept queerness within the brain's wiring as identity rather than a neurological problem. Deconstructing each of these characters with a "neuroqueer" eye allows us to rethink gender and neurological difference (as portrayed in *Star Trek* as simply artificial intelligence or alien difference) not as two disparate character traits, but as mutually inclusive.

Data is an android. He was constructed in his male creator's image. Because of the limits of cybernetics within *Star Trek*'s fiction, Data does not possess emotions. Data is coded as a superhuman autistic savant—a literal walking, talking supercomputer with unlimited access to boundless information, yet Data struggles to accomplish tasks as simple as understanding an offhand use of sarcasm. This is because Data is not part of the human system of signification; he does not belong in the human "signifying consciousness." Like in Barthes'[41] "Myth Today," to expand on his rose example: Data can learn that a rose signifies passion, but he cannot infer the meaning of a sign without first learning that the act of giving flowers is a sign of affection. A co-worker can tell Data their own connotative interpretation of the roses, and Data can remember and mimic their perspective; however, Data cannot come up with his own unique connotations. Data is a master of the denotative, but cannot grasp the connotative because of the way he is wired.

In the episode "In Theory"[42] of *The Next Generation*, one of Data's fellow engineering colleagues aboard the Enterprise, Jenna, attempts to start a romantic relationship with him. Although she is aware—as everyone else is—that Data does not possess emotions, she is shown to be visibly uncomfortable by Data's attempts to simulate romance. In one scene in particular, Jenna arrives unexpectedly at Data's quarters with a gift for him while he is painting. Data remarks on the unexpectedness of her visit, and Jenna responds, "I'm sorry, don't let me interrupt," clearly insinuating that she wishes for Data to stop what he is doing, rather than ignore her and return to his painting. To Jenna, Data's behavior is callous because he cannot understand the subtext in her language. But to Data—who learns through imitation and instruction—doing what someone tells him to do is the only way he is capable of showing respect. After their misunderstanding, Jenna remarks, "What matters is that you're trying." Data can simulate human displays of romance, but this doesn't mean he does not have his own legitimate way of showing affection. Throughout the episode, Data shows that he is very capable of being considerate to Jenna, as well as his friends and co-workers; even going as far as writing entire sub-routines within his programming specifically for interacting a certain way with a certain person.

This is a key in autistic affection: openly sharing information and creating information for another individual is a way of creating intimacy, the same way a neurotypical person shows it through flirtation and physical touch. Data's own struggle to understand connotation also carries over to Data's own perception of his gender. To Data, his body serves only as a vessel for him to interact with his surroundings. Data cannot infer the social value inherent in his fabricated appearance as an adult man. Data's autism manifests because he is an android created in the image of a human man, but because the signifier of "being" a man is empty. To Data, being a "man" doesn't denote a common identity, and this is evidently clear when you resist socialization.[43]

Heilker and Yergeau[44] bring up the concept of echolalia, a characteristic of some styles of autistic language use, characterized through "repeat[ed] stock words and phrases verbatim that they have heard other speakers use." Heilker and Yergeau identify that this trait has been dismissed by many who study the disorder as simply a meaningless parroting and even an impairment that should be overcome. They add that echolalia-like processes happen all the time in academia, in research, and through using citations; choosing to listen rhetorically "offers the possibility of generating a more productive discourse, a way to value autistic rhetoric and build upon it, rather than try to eradicate it." By recognizing Data's difference as something other than human through interpolation, the audience can realize their own social position in relation to the character. This forces the viewer to realize that they cannot fully empathize with Data, because his otherness cannot be willed away or fixed, as it is so concrete. This is how *Star Trek* effectively creates a space for rhetorical listening—by making Data less relatable to the audience by removing his humanity in a concrete way, he becomes easier to sympathize with than if he were simply an autistic human.

Dax is a lifeform(s) who is made up of the joining of a symbiont to a humanoid host, the former which has lived for hundreds of years in the bodies of many people of different genders. Jadzia, the Dax symbiont's current host, holds the collective consciousness and memories of all her previous hosts. Dax is inherently transgender because of her transient corporality; for Dax it is a part of her life cycle to switch bodies (and genders) once the host dies and the symbiont is joined with another. However, Dax's characterization differs from most popular examples of transgender characters in modern television shows. Cael M. Keegan[45] explores how transness is reconciled in *Degrassi: The Next Generation*, and the 2005 film *Transamerica*. Keegan notes the "manufacture of sympathy" with regards to the "pathologized position of trans people in society." The audience is manipulated to feel empathy for the transgender characters through symbolic representations of dysphoria—scenes that depict the character being exposed as performing a "fake gender" against their will, scenes of the transgender character scrutinizing their own body in a mirror. In Keegan's words, "the trans body is traditionally a tragic or melancholic body precisely because its gendered feelings cannot materialize in the world."

The struggle of being "alone" in one's own transness is necessary in the modern portrayals of transgender characters. *Star Trek* unintentionally opens a world of infinite transgender possibility. In a utopian future where "anything goes," where a transgender culture can thrive, Dax thrives because she is never alone; she is, quite literally, multiple people. In the episode "Facets"[46] of *Deep Space Nine*, Dax performs a ritual called zhian'tara, which allows her previous hosts to be transferred into the bodies of her colleagues temporarily and be communicated with. One of her previous hosts, Emony (inhabiting the body of the character Leeta), expresses that she was worried that being joined with the symbiont would affect her coordination, but later finds out that it actually improves her concentration, and Jadzia agrees. This mirrors the anxiety many transgender people harbor when deciding to transition medically; many worry that they will recognize the change as negative, but often, once transitioning, they find the change in hormones or body to be highly motivating and even euphoric. It is through exchanges like these that it is made clear that the process of changing bodies is a positive and enlightening experience for the character Dax.

Odo does not have a concrete form. He can imitate the form of other humanoids (albeit not very well) but can only do so for about a day before he must relax back into his liquid form. As an autistic coded character, Odo tries to imitate humanoid life, yet still remains an outsider because he is still imitating, and not truly "being." It causes him strain and discomfort to perform his humanoid identity for too long. Odo represents a character where transness and autism are interchangeable with one another. Like Dax, Odo also experiences corporality in a transient state. Odo's species naturally live a communal "hive mind," named the Link, as one being. On his own in *Deep*

*Space Nine* he is forced to imitate the conventions of humanoid living, like having a bipedal shape, having a purpose (a job), and having relationships with other people, despite it not being "natural" for him to do so. Like Data, Odo does not care about the implications of "being male," and it is likely he adopts the identity of maleness as a "default." As Susan Stryker[47] postulates on the performance of embodied gender: "the process of [transitioning] from one sex to another—renders visible the culturally specific mechanisms of achieving gendered embodiment." Odo's transformation from shapeless liquid to "male" humanoid reveals the viewers' own biases and socialized knowledge of maleness: why is Odo "male" if he has no chromosomes, has no genitalia? Odo does not even have internal organs. Why is Odo male simply because we are told he is? Odo takes humanoid form as a way of surviving in a society that doesn't accommodate his difference. So much of humanoid life depends on one's ability to touch/talk/interact with the world through the senses.

In the *Deep Space Nine* episode "The Alternate,"[48] Odo is reluctantly reunited with the scientist who studied him and ultimately "taught" him how to act as a humanoid. The station's bartender, Quark, jokes that Dr. Mora is Odo's father, implying that there is a paternal relationship between the two. Odo avoids eye contact with Mora, and is shown to be in discomfort with the situation. During a heated argument between the two, Dr. Mora says to Odo, "You would not be here today if it weren't for my guidance," implying that Odo is a lost cause or somehow less valuable as sentient life because he doesn't conform to Dr. Mora's expectations. Odo is a disabled and childlike subject for Dr. Mora to indoctrinate. This narrative is all too familiar when observing the narrative of parents of autistic children and hero complexes—the idea that autistic children owe any semblance of functionality and understanding of human interaction to their neurotypical parents. Dr. Mora is hyper-critical of Odo's "performance" of the humanoid figure, remarking that he hasn't quite perfected the shape of an ear. Other humanoids like Dr. Mora do not have to imitate humanoid shape, they simply are humanoid and are not questioned for it. Just as it is common for autistic people to struggle to conform socially, and for trans people to "pass," it is impossible for Odo to become solid; his "imitation" is never enough.

At the beginning of the series, Odo doesn't know that there are any other shapeshifters like him who exist. Odo's shapeshifting abilities are both respected because of their usefulness in his job as station head of security, and dismissed because they violently interrupt the illusion that he is humanoid. Odo expresses confusion at humanoid desires to have intimate relationships, to eat and drink, and to "have fun" like his peers, because he is not "wired" the same way as them. Odo later finds joy in exploring and fixating on his own talent of shapeshifting so much that he redesigns his own living space so that he can shapeshift into the various shapes around his room. At the end of the fourth season of *Deep Space Nine*, Odo is turned into a humanoid, removing his shapeshifting ability. It is the ultimate punishment for Odo's repeated failed performance of humanoid behavior. Odo is trapped inside a solid body that looks like his own imperfect simulacra of a human as a reminder that he will never quite fit in. His profound distress at this mirrors transgender and autistic discomfort of being forced into a body and/or forced to follow rigid social norms that go against their own identity. Odo experiences the discomfort of feeling hunger, thirst, and itchiness for the first time and is overwhelmed by these sensations that are commonly felt by other humanoids.

Much like the way female celebrities become icons for gay men through lack of proper representation, science fiction becomes a space for autistic viewers to imagine themselves within. It is not a coincidence that this is the most common stereotype associated with "high-functioning" autistics. Through the guise of speculative fiction, the modern constraints of gender, sexuality, and ability can be crossed safely without raising eyebrows. By creating alien characters with differences much more concrete and identifiable than the differences between humans, their inherent neurological queerness becomes more "believable." I can remember being a 14-year-old and wanting to become Data; it's strangely childish to have that kind of desire even as 14-year-old. There is a picture of me at Halloween from around that time; I feel humiliated when I look at it now, a decade later. I can remember realizing that putting on a costume that could be recognized as a symbol of how I felt about my own body and mind made me feel seen and understood. I remember how embarrassed I felt at myself for wanting to emulate a character rather than be a three-dimensional human being. To me, Data represents a character who doesn't have to embody his body. His failure to conform is accepted because he is a computer. Even in in my transgender, autistic adulthood, my echolalia manifests through the repeated reconciling and deconstruction of these characters I desperately identified with as a teenager.

---

*Gil Goletski is a multimedia doer from Vancouver, Canada. They make animation, cartoons, and music. They are always hydrated.*

# My Journey as a Transgender Woman with Autism

*Elizabeth K. Graham (she/her/hers)*

At the age of six months, I was adopted from East Asia by my loving parents; my mom was born and raised in the mid-West and was a musician and Sergeant Major in the US Army Band, and my dad was born and raised in New England and is the son of immigrants from China and does management consulting. The principal at my Montessori school suggested to my parents that I had a psychological evaluation, since she detected some learning differences. My mom also took me to a speech therapist for a few evaluation sessions. The evaluations revealed that I had learning needs that would not be best supported in a mainstream education setting. This prompted my parents to enroll me at The Lab School of Washington (LSW), a private school in northwest Washington DC that emphasizes art-based learning for students with moderate learning differences in grades 1–12. I was also born with Asperger's syndrome. The official diagnosis did not come until around my sophomore year in high school. When I learned of my diagnosis, everything made sense and I felt with this knowledge I could self-monitor and learn more about myself.

Throughout my years at LSW, as part of my individual education program, I received weekly group and one-to-one sessions from the school's in-house occupational therapists and speech and language therapists, and during high school with the clinical psychologists.

As I learned to express myself with others, I also began learning to play music. As a child, I was constantly enriched with the performing arts. From the start, my mom instilled in me a passion for playing music and we connected through music. I grew up listening to classical music and attending her concerts (and her colleagues' concerts) beginning at an early age. At around age seven years I started playing the piano, learning from my mom. Also, I began singing in my church's youth choir. I later switched over to the accordion in 1999 after seeing my mom's colleague play the accordion, and, fascinated by the instrument, I learned from him. From 2000 to 2004, I competed in accordion competitions across the country and participated in master classes with world-famous accordion players. I also took tap dancing classes during elementary school and performed in a couple of theater productions in high school.

Even as I was realizing I was different from others socially, I was also beginning to question the male gender I was born into, starting at around eight years of age. Growing up, I remember having more female friends over for play dates. In my tap dancing classes I was often the only boy and that didn't bother me. I went to Disney World in Orlando twice; on these trips I remember seeing the actors dressed up as Disney characters and I mostly gravitated toward characters such as Cinderella and Princess Jasmine. One Easter (I forgot the exact year but it was between 1997 and 2000) my mom got me a ceramic figure of an Easter bunny, but I was disappointed that it wasn't a girl Easter bunny and I wrote a letter to inform the Easter bunny of the mistake. My mom read the letter and reluctantly said, "I'll see if the store still has some." I think she said that to keep me calm because I don't remember her following up with me on this.

I didn't know how my family or friends would react to the fact I was questioning my gender identity, so I kept this a secret for a long time. Whenever I got the chance, whether it was when my mom was in the basement practicing or teaching music lessons or both of my parents were out of the house, I would take advantage of every moment I got and I would wear my mom's clothes and look at the clothing catalogues she received in the mail. When I was 11 or 12 years old, my mom caught me with her clothes in my room lying on the floor and she got upset. My dad was also upset. I felt too ashamed at the time to tell them the truth and for quite some time I didn't know any words to describe how I was feeling.

In December 2004, while in her 50s, my mom died from skin cancer, in my freshman year of high school. As is common with teenagers, I didn't spend a great amount of time with my mom, especially in the weeks leading up to her death. I felt sad for not having said I loved her enough or expressed enough how I was thankful for the music lessons and trips to the accordion competitions (especially after she began hospice care) but that was probably due to my expression challenges with Asperger's (prior to diagnosis). I have no siblings so I felt alone. My dad and I went to a couple of bereavement support groups and I met other teenagers experiencing similar losses, and this helped me realize that I wasn't the only teenager to experience this kind of loss. In these groups, I never discussed my questioning gender identity because I didn't know how to say it and I wasn't sure how other members and the group therapist would react.

My mom and I often bonded together on our annual summer cross-country trips to our family vacation home in the Rocky Mountains, stopping to visit my maternal grandparents on the way. My dad stayed back home and would take a flight out to meet us. We didn't have cable at home, so we watched a lot of movie channels on these trips; we often watched "chick flicks" together and my mom once commented on how most boys my age aren't interested in watching these movies. I didn't really react to that comment. Retroactively, I like to view this as our mother–daughter time.

In 2007, my dad enrolled me in the Georgetown University School of Continuing Studies College Preparatory Program, a non-credit summer program for high school students. For me, this was an opportunity to immerse myself in a mainstream academic setting, a social "dry run" if you will. I don't remember publicly disclosing to anyone my Asperger's diagnosis, but some of the teachers and other students were local so they knew about the Lab School. It was from this experience, interacting with mainstream peers, that I realized I could use more preparation to transition into a mainstream school. I felt I could benefit from a full school year at a mainstream school as a stepping stone. After graduating Lab School in 2008, I began my post-graduate year at a mainstream college preparatory boarding school in the eastern part of Pennsylvania, The Perkiomen School.

At Perkiomen, I began to involve myself in lesbian, gay, bisexual, transgender and questioning (LGBTQ) activities. I was among the founding members of the school's gay–straight alliance (GSA) to promote acceptance and understanding on campus. (I have learned that today many of the GSAs are now called "gender and sexuality alliances" to reflect the growing population of people of diverse sexual orientations and gender identities.) A few weeks before graduation at Perkiomen, I confided in a fellow classmate and friend (at the time) that I was a closeted transgender woman. As is common with people on the autism spectrum, I trusted her completely; I shared with her some photos of myself in women's clothing. Unfortunately, those photos got into the hands of another student who sent the photos to the entire student body. I found out about this through the dean of students; he called me into his office one night during study hall and told me what had happened and what was being done to handle the situation. I told him that I was not out to my dad and he respected my request for discretion. As I walked the hallways back to my dorm, I could hear laughter from the other students.

A couple of days later, the student responsible for the spreading of the photos was identified and expelled. I am thankful to the dean of students, faculty, and fellow members of the school's GSA who were kind to me throughout this situation. I have kept in touch with some of my former classmates on Facebook and saw some of them for the first time at my first Perkiomen Alumni gathering in Washington, DC in 2016; they all said that I was looking great. As a woman of God, I prayed for that student; I still pray that he has or will realize the impact of his actions and the impact of transphobia.

Shortly thereafter, I was accepted to the Marshall University College Program for Students with Autism Spectrum Disorder (CPSASD) for enrollment in fall 2009. (I found the CPSASD while doing an online search at Perkiomen for support for college students with Asperger's.) I earned my bachelor's degree in psychology and minored in counseling, focusing on bereavement in people on the autism spectrum. I took counseling and sociology classes relating to death and bereavement. I also did a clinical observation at the local hospice as part of my counseling minor with patients, support groups, and a bereavement camp for families. My big project was writing a paper on bereavement in people on the autism spectrum, which I presented at the 2013 Marshall University College of Liberal Arts Conference as well as in a plenary session at the Tri-State Psychology Conference at the University of Charleston in West Virginia. I then went on to present this paper at the Autism Society's National Conference in Pittsburgh in July 2013.

At Marshall University, I was involved with different student organizations. During my freshman year, I was active in the student LGBTQ group, helping to educate the campus community on transgender issues and helping with safe-space training. I performed my accordion in the drag show on campus in spring 2010. Beginning my sophomore year, I became an active volunteer with the campus blood drives. I am a regular blood donor, influenced by my mom donating blood in the wake of the 9/11 attacks and seeing other cancer patients receive blood transfusions. I used this passion of mine to connect with other blood donors and establish the Marshall University

American Red Cross Club. I have found socializing and connecting with others is easier when there is an already established mutual interest. However, given my name being in the school newspaper a lot to promote the blood drives and the issues with blood donation with the LGBTQ community at the time (and that I was not openly transgender), I kept my involvement with campus LGBTQ activities low profile. I was also involved with Marshall's chapter of Students Against Destructive Decisions (SADD) and served as the secretary in my senior year. Shortly before graduation in May 2013, Dean of Student Affairs Steve Hensley presented me with the Outstanding Service to Marshall University award.

On returning home to the Washington DC area, I wanted to use my personal experience with autism spectrum disorder (ASD) to support people with intellectual or developmental disabilities (I/DD). In October 2013, I began working as a direct support professional at an agency that provides community-based residential supports to adults with I/DD; I supported adults who live in their own homes as well as those living in staff-supported group homes. At this agency, I also helped to lead a program that helps young adults with ASD and I/DD transition from high school to adult life through helping to teach cooking and social skills classes.

While I was beginning my professional career, I was also considering my strategy for transitioning. In August 2014, I had moved out of my dad's house and begun living with roommates; this gave me the time and space I needed to evaluate my decision to transition. In 2015, after seeing a therapist for a while to help me decide if transitioning was the right choice, I decided that a new job would help me get a fresh start and beginning my transition soon would be best. Remembering my classmate spreading my photos and the reaction from my parents when I was young, I was wary of how people might react. I first came out to friends from church, high school, and college. I decided to come out to my dad on my 26th birthday on August 16, 2015. (All four of my grandparents had died in their 80s and 90s by the time I graduated high school.) He said he loved me and that he was not too surprised. He told me that he and my mom were having discussions with each other relating to this when I was younger. My dad said seeing Caitlyn Jenner's award speech in July helped him in understanding, so I believe my timing was great. My dad's partner, the woman he is now seeing, said she would continue to love and support me.

For a brief period, I did part-time driving for Uber and Lyft. One night I got the courage to drive as my real self. On one ride to the airport, the passenger kept looking at me through the rearview mirror. It wasn't until later I realized I had forgotten to update my profile photo. I began to realize how open and accepting people are becoming these days of those of different gender identities. Prior to my legal name change, there were plenty of passengers who kindly called me Elizabeth when I asked. Although coming out to strangers is different from doing so with family, this did help me prepare coming out to family and other friends. After the legal aspects of my transition were completed I was happy to share my story with passengers who were open and they often found my journey very interesting to the extent where the ride was too short.

Shortly after coming out I began attending transgender support group therapy sessions and receiving hormone treatment at Whitman-Walker Health in Washington DC, a clinic well known for supporting the medical and behavioral health needs of the LGBTQ community. I received and took my first doses of testosterone blockers and estrogen pills on Thursday, November 5, 2015. Whitman-Walker also provides periodic gender/name change clinics and helped me in 2016 with the documents and letters to update my name and gender marker on my Social Security card, driver's license, and passport book and passport card. (To get a fresh new start, I decided to change my full name.) Attending the support group therapy sessions was helpful and made me feel less alone in my journey.

I also became active again in 2016 in the church where I grew up, Westmoreland Congregational United Church of Christ (UCC) located in Bethesda, Maryland. On Easter weekend 2016, I received in the mail the court order for my full legal name change; the timing was nice with Easter. My congregation has been supportive of me in my transition. I have spoken at a couple of church events about my transition; this helped with the congregation's decision in adding "gender identity" to its Open and Affirming statement. (Open and Affirming is the UCC's designation of a congregation being welcoming to members and clergy of different gender identities and sexual orientations.) I also was elected to my congregation's Board of Spiritual Formation. I also got involved with the United Church of Christ Potomac Association LGBTQ network, helping to represent the group in Capital Pride Festivals. I also became connected to local transgender community members and groups.

I was offered and accepted the position in November 2015 of a service coordinator for the Maryland Waiver for Children with Autism at The Arc of Prince George's County. Despite interviewing in September 2015 as my former male self, I came out to my boss in an email shortly after accepting the job offer to disclose that I was planning to begin my transition. To my relief, my supervisor and her supervisor said that my transition would be a non-issue. My gender transition with my job transition went quite seamlessly.

In October 2017, I visited Marshall and my friends in the CPSASD for the family reception and breakfast during homecoming weekend. It was great to see my friends, professors, and mentors from my college days. It was also great to meet some of the current students and their families. Back when I was at Marshall as a student, I would dress up in women's clothes and walk around campus after dark, sometimes with a couple of close friends in whom I had confided. This was not only the first time returning as an alumna, but the first time since beginning my transition. It felt liberating to be back on campus as my true self during daylight; when I re-introduced myself to one of my psychology professors, he said he couldn't recognize me (and I took this as a compliment). I am thankful to my friends from Marshall University for supporting me through my time in the closet.

As a transgender woman, I do face challenges. I am sometimes self-conscious of people noticing that I am a transgender woman and how they will react. I have got better with my voice and I am misgendered less these days over the phone, when my face isn't seen, or at the fast food drive-thru. I have also been working on my alto voice and I have sung once in my church's chancel choir. Dating can be a challenge, especially with men; I don't disclose that I am transgender right away, but I will disclose prior if we plan on meeting. Right now, I feel security in online dating because of this.

I have often asked myself that if my mom was still alive, would she accept me as her daughter, if she knew she was adopting a late-blossoming daughter. The greatest challenge for me so far with my transition has been my mom's absence. While my mom was in the hospice I had a few moments in private with her. I apologized one last time for a few things. However, I didn't tell her that I felt deep down that I was a girl. I felt that this would have been the perfect time to tell her but at the same time the timing didn't feel right. On the night of May 22, 2018, I had dreamt the moment I had longed for. I and my mom and dad were at her childhood home. I would like to point out the dream was present day. I had come back in from walking someone to the front door. We were having an emotional discussion about some sort of medical procedure for her. They were talking to me about putting me on a flight back home to Washington. I remember saying that I wasn't returning home until she was done with the procedure. I gave Mom a hug and immediately I felt like I was actually hugging her while she was wearing the hospital gown she was wearing when she was in hospice care back in 2004. (The Thursday or Friday before the Monday my mom died, she said to me,

"I love you" as I walked out the door to school and this was the last day she was awake and talking; these were the last words my mom said to me before she died.) And in this dream, when we hugged, she said to me, "I love you, Elizabeth." I began to cry. I then woke up from the dream, shaking and crying. It was about 12:30 in the middle of the night. This was the first dream I had had with my mom in it (at least clearly and remembering it) since taking hormones in November 2015. That dream gave me the answers to my questions.

As I continue to help people with autism and I/DD and with my involvement with the LGBTQ community, I am constantly reminded of my own experience. I am reminded that there are individuals with I/DD who are transgender and do not have the same early intervention and loving acceptance I've been blessed with. I'm very thankful to God for a wonderful and supporting family and group of friends.

---

*Elizabeth began to realize her gender at age eight and, although not diagnosed with Asperger's until years later, this began her journey with loss, bullying, autism, and becoming a woman.*

# Face the Strange

*Dan Ackerman (they/them/theirs)*

Born in 1991, I was late to the Bowie game. People loved him for decades before I was born, to an astronomical degree. They loved him enough to make his influence so pervasive that I adored him before I even knew who he was. His songs were everywhere and once I put a name to the voice I had to stop and go "This is him, too?" for dozens of songs I'd loved since childhood.

For the past few years, the people who know me best have given me Bowie-themed gifts. I have a giant, framed poster that I bought at the V&A David Bowie Is... exhibition. I have shirts, I have coloring books, movies, albums, and anthologies that analyze his work. David Bowie is my special interest (and I don't mean I'm trying to lobby Congress for anything).

The term might ring familiar for those of you with autism or who know more than most about autism spectrum disorder (ASD). A special interest, for an autistic person (a person like me), is something they love with an intensity most people don't have for hobbies or celebrities or things. They might know everything about the topic, they might have an expansive collection of something, or they might pursue their hobby relentlessly for hours.

There is nothing about him I don't love. I wilfully ignore the bad things, like when people say his queerness was all an act, that he was just playing to the fags and freaks to make money or when they dredged up the under-aged girls in the wake of his death or when other artists claim he ripped them off. I am not here to judge a man for his actions, I am here to tell you what David Bowie, as an artist, meant to me.

I have always been a human lacking humanity, someone on the fringe of society looking in and not understanding what anyone was doing or why they were doing it. The real world has always been something I couldn't quite touch. It was over there with the rest of you, and I was here in my head, alone. Social situations are nuanced, complicated, and torturous. I have scripts to follow for small talk, but when things go sideways, my heart starts to race. I am disconnected, lonely, and resentful. I don't like people because they are confusing and veiled; I want friends, real friends to talk to and spend time with, but I just can't figure out how to make them. Who can you hang out with, is it weird to be pals with your married, 40-something co-worker? Is it wrong to call your cat your best friend? What about when the person you want to spend time with the most is one of the students you work with, because talking to a seven-year-old is your cut-off for understanding social communication?

Every interaction, every outing (not every one but it feels like all of them) is nothing but frayed nerves and wanting to go home, to be done with all of this, but then, at home, wanting someone to be with you. I'm not totally alone, I have a family, I have pets, I'm married, but even when I'm with those who are closest to me, I know I'm not normal. There's a vast gulf between me and other people; I'm standing on one side trying to reach over and sometimes I find someone who's willing to reach back and make contact. They love me, but they don't understand. They don't understand the anxiety, the routines, the need for stability, and the inability to provide it for myself; they don't understand the meltdowns when things are too much and they don't understand how hard I try to seem like them, to hide the freakishness of my inner life.

I go to one gas station and I go there on my way to work (or from work if it's an emergency). I have two back-up gas stations I can go to if it's a real emergency because the threat of being stranded is worse than the discomfort of going somewhere different. When I first learned to drive, I had one gas station and I always asked my boyfriend to pump the gas with me. Even now, I can't remember the last time I went to the grocery store or the mall alone. In order to try new foods, I have to mull the idea over for months, watch other people eat it, ask a thousand questions about how it is and even then, when the moment comes and I bring it to my lips, it still might end up in the trash (or the dog's bowl) untasted.

The people around me cannot understand that my body is not my body. A body should feel like home and mine feels like a prison in a thousand different ways. My body does not look the way it should, it does not react to stimuli the way it should. I do not love my body, and not just because I don't like the way I look but because I am uncomfortable. I like myself best when I am hurting (squeezing, biting, tearing my cuticles, thumping my chest, hitting my head, cutting, burning) because that, at least, I understand. I live my life tangled up in flesh when I should be floating in space, when I should be something that looks as Other as I feel.

Even among other trans people, my gender is less real. Even among other queer people, my identity is fraught and nuanced and sometimes just plain "made up." I cannot call myself autistic openly because I do not have the right pieces of paper to tell the world that my diagnosis is not just real but valid. I cannot get that diagnosis without a hefty bill and even then, what would it get me? Medical validity? The label "high-functioning"? People telling me "but you're not really autistic, though?" Denial, negation, special treatment, awareness?

Not understanding. Not acceptance.

Maybe you know where I'm going with this.

Bowie was a beacon for the freaks, for the weirdos, those who didn't fit in. He was an alien among us, thin and pale, eerie and beautiful. He was something else, something not of this world. He was like me because he didn't belong here either.

He was nervous, awkward in interviews (the cocaine, I know), and his songs felt just as lonely as I did. He seemed to understand that life is painful and joyous at the same time. He was the mask of another man, a man called David Jones, who lived a private, quiet life with his family.

The things he did were weird. And not just fashion-forward weird or cute and quirky weird. Songs-about-gnomes weird. Mimes weird. In the unapologetic beauty of his weirdness, I could construct a vision of myself that was not disgusting, unlovable, and in need of fixing.

When I saw Bowie in all his freakish glory, I was able to, for the first time, understand that it was okay to be the way I am.

He is my god, my hero. I knew, even before he died, that I would never know him, that we would never meet and that our worlds were vastly different. But, in my head, we're on a first-name basis.

---

*Dan Ackerman is a queer, trans autistic author, and an educator. They hope to provide representation and advocate for the rights of marginalized people.*

# Ableism in Poetry

*Kaiden Cole Wilde (he/him/his)*

## ABLEISM IN THE ROOM

There are 4 hard rules in slam poetry—
one of them is:
the poet may not use props.

No props in slam poetry...

now,
not knowing if there's a strict definition of props
in this situation...
I think to myself,
well shit.
Slam poetry just became inaccessible
to me and every other autistic or disabled poet I know.

I mean it's in the slam motto: "poetry is the point"
but how many poets are silenced by the no-prop rule?

I wonder
how many
inaccessible things
will I want to do in my lifetime?

I cannot name that kind of pain without prompt,
without a paper in front of me—
I think
it is something like
violence
or discrimination—

or, oh wait, I've got it:
Ableism.

Maybe
it's not really a big deal though,
I mean there are worse forms of ableism—

So let's go back to the definition of a prop:

Something that props or sustains;

SUPPORT.

Well shit, then I guess a wheelchair is a prop,
I guess a cane is a prop,
I guess a communication device for a non-speaking poet is a prop
I guess my turtle plushie is
a prop—
and it's fucked up that I have to make him into a prop
to show you he isn't one.

Because if a prop is something that supports,
and poets can't use props,
then I can't be a poet.

Society already pushes disabled folks into able-bodied molds,

so determined to call a speaking autistic "high-functioning"
and tell the non-speaking autistics they're shit out of luck—

and for the record,
we fucking hate functioning labels.

In my community, those have no meaning.

Autistics are defined by our humanity,
and all humans need support sometimes.

That's one of the beautiful things about being human.

And there are worse forms of ableism, I guess.

Like how my stepfather called me retarded
while I stood still as a statue under the pressure of sensory overload
in the middle of the grocery store.

Like how people treat me different when my autism becomes
    visible—
how suddenly, my worst moments are how my worth is measured.

Like how my lover is seen as a caretaker,
how it is assumed that they must be neurotypical
and how suddenly everyone knows our relationship better than we do.

Hear me out:
It's not scary to walk through your house in pitch darkness if you
    trust yourself...

but it is scary to be told that the most intrinsic part of your
    identity is undesirable—
to stare at your own brown eyes in the mirror at eight years old to
    practice "good eye contact"
and still not be good at it,
and to be told you have to be good at it if you ever want to succeed
which is a euphemism for "live a happy life,"
because so much of happiness is dependent upon success

and I am not good
at it.

Ableism
is no props in slam poetry.

As if Bellamy the baby sea turtle is optional—
if he were really a prop,
I might throw him on the ground for dramatic effect
but to do so would be to harm myself.

I too have been a prop,
been harmed for dramatic affect—
just watch *Rain Man*, *The Big Bang Theory*, *The Accountant*, or *Atypical*.

I have too often felt my support
stripped from me.

You see I need to feel the beads underneath my fingertips,
with only his velvety belly skin between them.

---

*Kaiden Cole Wilde is a transmasculine and autistic poet with a passion for activism and advocacy. Intersectionality is at the heart of all that he does and cares about. His body of work covers many topics in this realm that have affected him personally, including his queer identity, and experiences with disability, poverty, and trauma.*

# The Realest Parts of Me

*Devin S. Turk (he/him/his or they/them/theirs)*

In the winter of 1997, my parents hung a pink and white banner in the kitchen window of our townhouse to announce my arrival to the world: "IT'S A GIRL!" From the outsider's perspective looking in on my life growing up, I seemed to be a typically developing girl with a good home life. As a child, I excelled at school and on the softball field. I loved arts and crafts. I was a Girl Scout. But this is not the entire truth. For starters, from the age of eight through my teenage years, my parents were involved in an extremely high-conflict divorce and a very stressful legal custody battle. I was also somewhat socially withdrawn, painfully shy, and easily brought to tears, especially when confronted by new people and unfamiliar environments. My adolescence was one that consisted of panic attacks, social isolation, and many months spent in psychiatric hospitals. When I was 14, I was diagnosed with Asperger's syndrome (now autism spectrum disorder), yet it took roughly six years of internal consideration before I began to be openly vocal about being autistic. At the time, my diagnosis was met with skepticism from some people close to me, and my identity as an autistic person was subsequently stifled and written off as something that had been falsified.

These days, I think about how vastly different my life would have been (and would still be today) if there was less dissonance between my internal and external worlds. The first way I was aware of this misalignment manifesting in my life was via my pre-transition body. As a younger teen, I spent hours watching and re-watching vlogs by transmasculine people on YouTube. I searched the internet for all of the "one year on testosterone" video montages and top surgery reveals I could find online. "Maybe someday...maybe," I thought to myself. Now, at 21 years old, I am about three-and-a-half years on testosterone gel and one year post-op from my own top surgery. Feeling the spring breeze on my flat, bare chest is one of my favorite things in the world. I want to point out, though, that I do not consider my transition to be some kind of "female to male" linearity with a definite ending point. I am non-binary, and my "transition" is a perpetual process, like any kind of personal betterment. There is always more to learn about myself and ways I can work towards living a life that is more and more aligned with who I want to be and who I am.

When I think of my personal path to self-acceptance, I marvel at how two main aspects of my personhood (my autistic-ness and my transness) can be vastly different while still occupying similar themes. For me, being autistic and being trans each come with the societal hurdles of stigma and lack of general public knowledge about what it's like to inhabit a marginalized identity. I can easily imagine spaces in which I would feel both emotionally and physically unsafe because of the ways I am, whether or not other people know about them. But because of the ways our society largely acknowledges neither gender diversity nor neurodiversity, I am also prone to feeling doubly invisible. My years of taking testosterone have rendered me cis-male-assumed by those who don't know me, and two decades of learning to socially camouflage myself have disguised my neurotype behind a persona that is built on what I think people want to see in me. I wonder about what it would be like if more of me was visible in plain sight.

Like many autistic people, I utilize the social adaptation technique known as "masking." Like a chameleon that changes color in the hope of hiding from predators, an autistic person such as myself may stifle or cover up their natural body language and other ways of expressing themselves so that they might be perceived as more neurotypical.

For me, much of wearing a mask involves observing the individuals in my environment so I can mirror or copy their postures, gestures, and tones of voice. It also involves suppressing urges to stim in ways that are obviously autistic, like flapping my hands or rocking back and forth.

*Side note: I believe it is important to acknowledge that I view my ability to mask as a double-edged sword. Even though it often negatively affects my mental health beyond belief, I am aware that I hold a kind of privilege. If my surroundings were to include people who could possibly be hostile in response to my autistic-ness, I would be able to be to utilize masking and secure my safety without much suspicion. I am aware that this is simply not a reality for every autistic person.*

While putting on a polite face in the presence of others is likely something many non-autistics can also relate to, I know my degree of social camouflaging is unhealthy. Even just 30 minutes of chatting with a friend at a coffee shop can leave me feeling utterly exhausted and depressed because of how much I had been altering myself to be considered neurotypical in someone else's eyes. It's not unusual for me to need to lie down in a dark room by myself for several hours after socializing. It's my body's message to my brain telling me that my masking isn't natural; it's an artificial presentation of myself that takes a lot of mental energy to uphold. And yet I feel *compelled* to mask. I feel like I *have* to copy other people so that I don't stand out. It is not necessarily for safety reasons, but because of how I've internalized the ways our society talks about and treats those who deviate from the norm...whatever the "norm" is. I most definitely know there's nothing "bad" about being visibly queer or neurodivergent, but many years of socialization in this ableist and queerphobic world have urged me to think that difference is undesirable. That difference must be apologized for, and it is to be extinguished. Consciously, of course, I know all of that is dangerously toxic rhetoric. That kind of thinking by our society is what keeps people like me from holding their true power in their own two hands.

Currently, I'm immersing myself in autistic advocacy culture as much as is humanly possible. I'm immeasurably grateful for all of the resources I've discovered via the internet. There are great organizations out there doing intersectional work I admire, such as the Autistic Self Advocacy Network, Autistic Women & Nonbinary Network, and Thinking Person's Guide to Autism. I'm a frequent lurker and participator in various online autistic communities like the weekly Autchat discussions on Twitter, the #ActuallyAutistic hashtag, movements like Red Instead, and countless Facebook groups. I'm currently reading *Neurotribes: The Legacy of Autism and the Future of Neurodiversity* by Steve Silberman, *Loud Hands: Autistic People, Speaking* by The Loud Hands Project, and *Authoring Autism: On Rhetoric and Neurological Queerness* by Melanie Yergeau. I'm soaking in everything I can about my people: our histories, our politics, our pride, and the injustices we face as a community and as individuals.

When I took the same approach in reference to my trans identity, I learned a simple yet invaluable lesson: everyone's story is different, and one story cannot speak for all others. The same goes for autistics and folks who are otherwise neurodivergent. My life experiences are not necessarily unique to me, but my story is and should be respected as such. So, where do I go from here? While only time can tell, I already see how claiming agency over, and being vocal about, *both* my autistic neurotype and my queer/trans identity—and the ways in which they intersect—have begun to shape me into a fuller, more confident version of myself. I look forward to embodying even more authenticity. I'm excited to see what this will bring and where it will take me, and ultimately, where it will take *us*.

---

*Devin S. Turk is an autistic, non-binary university student in northern Virginia. He enjoys photography, writing poetry, and spending time with his beloved cat, Arthur.*

# Neuroccino

## The Life and Times of an Autistic Trans Man Working at Dunkin' Donuts

*Nathaniel Glanzman (he/him/his)*

The more I descend into sensory overload, the more the Oasis Machine blender sounds like speaker feedback. It feels like my gray matter is being ground up with somebody's cotton candy coolatta, the blood-brain barrier bursting and filling the blended sugar water with chopped up lobotomy scraps. The oven beeps are car alarms, the overhead bulbs police lights. I stop myself from screaming into my headset and say:

"Thank you for choosing Dunkin'. What can I get started for you?"

"I need a large iced coffee with extra, extra caramel. Caramel in the cup, extra sugar, extra pumps of caramel and extra whipped cream. No ice."

"So, like, a cup of caramel with a drop of coffee in it?"

"You're in no position to judge. Last time, you people forgot to give me two extra cups of ice. Think about that before you decide to be smart, young lady."

I'm trying to separate all of this from the song that's playing in the lobby. I think it's "California Girls," but nobody knows for sure. It could have been "Down with the Sickness" and I would have heard Snoop Dogg rapping about squeezing people.

I haven't told my co-workers that I'm trans or autistic, but something tells me they already know. I'm a short, pudgy, feminine-faced, wide-eyed half-Filipino who infodumps about psychology and always carries a fidget spinner in his pocket. Wearing a binder and nodding when people speak doesn't fool anybody.

I count pumping a cup halfway full with caramel as arm day and send it off to the poor bastard who has to ring up for this woman, who I call The Caramel Lady. I think about what it's like to make eye contact with her soulless orbs and I cringe.

I realize when The Caramel Lady drives away that I forgot to put coffee in it, but I doubt she'll notice.

BEEP!

"Thank you for choosing Dunkin'." Get started for what? I...I mean...!

"Oh, don't worry, sweetie. It's been a long day. I would like a medium almond milk iced latte with two pumps of sugar-free vanilla, three and a half extra shots and exactly twelve ice cubes."

"Of course. I'll have that for you as soon as I can translate that into English."

"Thank you, ma'am! Don't work too hard!"

"You too."

As soon as I say that, I feel like squirting Spic and Span in my eyes. Maybe the excruciating pain will make my voice deeper.

Then, there is a customer at the counter.

I force myself to make eye contact and my brown irises are punctured with blue. He is a middle-aged white man with a newspaper under his arm and a smile that I cannot decipher. His wrinkles meander like rivers and delta at his eyelids. I count his liver spots. He has four of them on his left hand.

"Grabbed somebody else's name tag when you were in a rush, huh?" He asks with a grin.

While he is congratulating himself for being friendly, I go nonverbal. I open my mouth briefly, but no sound escapes me. It is like all of the words I wish to say are being held back with a fishhook inside my throat. My eyes well with tears when I realize that if my name tag had said, "Kelly" or "Brittany" he wouldn't have batted an eye.

"That is his name, actually," my co-worker asserts, going back to cleaning the milk machine as if he hadn't said anything.

I marvel at his confidence, and am again at a loss for words. The fishhook is preventing me from thanking him.

"Oh, heh. Of course," the customer says, digging out his wallet to give a one-dollar tip out of penance.

"I-It's okay. I get that a lot," I say, my words finally unthawing.

What he doesn't know is this is actually a lie. Most of the time, people just label me a girl and make that their reality.

I could have made his drink with my eyes closed: a medium hot coffee with regular cream and sugar. I float on clouds and make sure that the lid is secured extra tightly. Even though I was misgendered, this person had made the effort to correct his mistake. I could count on one hand the number of times that had happened to me at work.

I hand him his coffee with a warm smile, not making direct eye contact. He takes it and says:

"I didn't mean anything by that, man."

I sputter something to the effect of "Don't worry about it" and he leaves. I am filled with an indescribable warmth and repeat his words to myself like a looped YouTube video. For every time that I am called "ma'am" that day, I think back to him saying "man" and smile like a dork.

---

*Nathaniel Glanzman is a Virginia-based high school English teacher whose special interests include psychology, neuroscience, and Beyblade. He reads the DSM for fun.*

# My Gender Is Yenn:
# A Coming Out Story

Yenn Purkis (they/them/their)

I have known that I have not conformed to the expected gender "norms" for many years. I have also known I was somehow "different" since childhood. I was first diagnosed as autistic in 1994 when I was 20 but I have only recently affirmed that I am non-binary.

Looking back at my life there are clear indications of my gender identity from when I was very small. One of the rudest taunts from school bullies involved my ambiguous gender. I didn't really understand what the issue was. The insult "Are you a boy or a girl?" only hurt me because I knew it was intended to hurt me. The idea of not knowing which binary gender "spot" I fitted in didn't particularly concern me. If I ever thought about it I viewed my gender as "me." As I was growing up there was little understanding of gender diversity. My dad's cousin was trans so I knew that trans was an option but didn't really refer that to myself at the time. The gender "options" I knew about seemed bound up with sexuality rather than gender. The view that androgynous women must be lesbians and that sort of thing. There was no real discussion in society of the many different kinds of gender identity until I was well into adulthood. I assumed I must be female because that was my assigned gender at birth but it never sat well with me.

I remembered the times I got in trouble for taking my top off as a child, thinking the only reason women kept their shirts on was that they had breasts but I did not at the age of eight. I was totally affronted by getting in trouble for doing something that seemed natural to do on a hot day and which the boys—who also didn't have breasts—could do with impunity! In my teen and young adult years I remember seeing outwardly cisgender women in heels, makeup, and fascinators and thinking they must have somehow been brainwashed to be so girly!

Fast forward several years to 2018. I have become an author and presenter on all things autism. I have a big following among autistic people and others within the autism community. I have become something of a "brand" and my outward expression is quirky, fun and individual—rainbow wigs, sequin shoes, and lots of color. I also have a large circle of trans and gender-diverse autistic friends.

I started to consciously reflect on my gender identity over the past 12 months. I realized that my outward expression has gone from shaved hair, "men's" clothes, and work-boots in my youth to more traditionally "feminine" and then to my expression now which is more about playing with notions of gender and expectations around being autistic. I have never really identified with binary female or male notions of identity.

I talked to some of my friends about my new understanding of my gender. It felt "right" to be non-binary but in fact I was still closeted. In June 2019 I posted this on my Facebook profile page:

I recently publicly affirmed and declared that I identify as being of non-binary gender and that I prefer being referred to as "them/they" to being "she/her." It has been incredibly liberating and opening new possibilities to my understanding of myself and others. It makes me feel sort of young, like I am discovering more about myself than I knew was there. I am wondering why it took me so long to get to this point of identifying and understanding. There is a lot of contented happy wandering through life tempered by occasional worry and uncertainty.

Coming out—and doing it so publicly—was a far bigger step than I thought it would be. I imagined that coming out would just be an affirmation of something I already knew but that was far from the case. My coming out was many things, but mostly it was a liberation.

I started to consciously play with my identity. My worries centered around that fraught idea of "going through a phase." This struck me as very strange given my years in the queer community arguing against that kind of thinking when it was applied to others. I guess anxiety isn't often very logical. I eventually arrived at the knowledge that I was 43 and knew my mind but even if I didn't, why did it matter? Surely people go through different points in life in terms of other elements of their identity. It just seems that gender diversity and sexuality are areas where it is apparently okay to invalidate someone's experience by saying it is "a phase."

Another issue I had was that I found it really hard to stop misgendering myself for a while, which was both very frustrating and kind of poignant when friends apologized for accidentally misgendering me! It took around three months to get to a point where I didn't regularly misgender myself. I hardly ever do it now, which is a relief! The reason for unintentionally misgendering myself was that I had identified as "she/her" for 43 years! It was pretty much the same issue that respectful friends have through knowing me as one gender and then needing to change my pronouns having always used the pronouns that I have left behind.

Not all friends have been respectful of my affirmed identity or pronouns. Some people flatly refused to use "they/them," giving a variety of excuses from "I am old and I don't know about this stuff" and "that is just fashion." Those sorts of responses upset me and feed into my already existing sense of self-doubt. They are a cruel thing.

I suppose that might be why those people say things like that. Other people just either ignore or "forget" that I use they/them and call me she, girl, woman... I don't know their intent without stating my identity again and potentially forcing a difficult conversation. I am not afraid of difficult conversations but I have a limit and this issue occurs frequently. I wish just being able to be my own happy, non-binary me wasn't seen by others as being so political! I don't want to spend my life correcting people and educating people because it is stressful and I feel that I shouldn't have to do that but then I also don't want to be misgendered for the rest of my life either!

A friend who is trans and non-binary told me shortly after I came out that I would find out who my friends were. They were absolutely correct. Some of the people I expected to be judgmental and bigoted surprised me by being wonderful and respectful. Conversely, I lost some online "friends" who I would never have thought would behave that way. I also got a lot of random bigoted trolling from strangers. I posted some video diaries about my coming out on YouTube. The second of these seems to have attracted rent-a-troll as I had around 20 people tell me that my gender identity was a mental illness and that I was trying to corrupt children and so forth. It was extremely hurtful. I posted a video diary entry shortly afterwards talking about how trolling around gender is so damaging (and I turned off the comments function!). I keep finding reminders that being non-binary is seen by others as a political act rather than simply being how I am.

In fact, there is a positive around the political nature of how trans and gender-diverse people experience life. My being an autistic advocate who is non-binary opens a lot of doors for other people, validating them and helping them to build their sense of who they are. In the five months since I came out, I have had a load of autistic people message me to say they realized they are also non-binary after reading and watching my work about autism and gender. Yes, it appears that I am a gender whisperer! I feel very strongly accepted and included in the autism and trans and gender-diverse community. Given that I spent my childhood and teens and early adult life essentially alone, this is a great thing and something I wish to all who want and need it.

So many autistic people are trans/gender diverse but like me, some people don't realize this until later in their life. I love that my being a reasonably well-known autistic person who is non-binary has allowed others to find who they are, because finding who you are is a great thing.

My coming out has had impacts for me beyond gender. It has cemented my identity. I finally know who I am—or I think I do! My self-esteem and confidence are beyond anywhere they have been before. Before I came out, I had a lot of insecurity, which resulted in me comparing myself to others—never a good idea. I would always be on edge at autism events, worrying that everyone else was somehow "better" than me at advocacy or whatever. Since about two weeks after coming out this has ceased to be an issue. I know, accept, and value who I am. This is a wonderful unexpected gift.

I have also been asked to do things in the lesbian, gay, bisexual, transgender, queer or questioning, intersex, and asexual or allied (LGBTQIA+) and autism space. I am on an LGBTQIA+ steering committee for an autism organization and was recently featured in an amazing video called *Autistic Ways of Gender*, alongside several other autistic people, many of whom are trans and gender diverse.

I was part of a webinar called "Autistic LGBTIQ+ and Proud" for Australian autism mentoring organization the I CAN Network earlier this year. Three of the other people on the panel were under 25. One was 17. I see a clear generational difference in attitudes around gender between people my age and 20-somethings and teens. While there is still a very long way to go, it was amazing to share the virtual stage with people who were that switched on and who understand levels of nuance about gender it has taken me a lot longer to learn. There was such a sense of pride—queer and autistic. A few older people in the webinar commented that Dr. Wenn Lawson (also on the panel) and myself should be able to retire from advocacy soon as the young people would be fine to keep on changing the world! I felt so proud for our community. It made me think that things must be going in the right direction.

Coming out was a huge thing for me. It has shifted my perspective and made my life better. However, this brings some thoughts to mind. I am an optimist. In the Yenn universe, diversity continues to be more respected over time until we do not need to do much other than enjoy our lovely inclusive world. But I know that this probably isn't going to be the case.

Everything we have is up for grabs. Times change and different people have influence on thinking. We live in a society where opinion on matters of diversity—including autism and gender—is very divided. I live in my happy little bubble where bigotry is rare and I am supported to address it, but not everyone lives in that world.

In 2017, there was a plebiscite—basically a survey—in Australia about whether marriage laws should be changed to include gay and lesbian couples. Thankfully the result was a resounding "YES!" and I am enjoying attending friends' weddings now, yet the messaging from bigoted people and groups in the time leading up to the decision was loud and awful. Even in my own experience, I had three friends, including a 13-year-old child, who were physically attacked by bigoted strangers because they did not clearly fit into expectations of gender. There are a lot of bigots out there and they are just as keen to preach hatred and roll back gains as we are to change things to be more inclusive, respectful, and generally nicer. And transphobic comments from world leaders just make this battle harder.

We cannot be complacent in this area. Anyone who knows me knows I am not much of a radical. Someone even described my activism as "cuddly" but I do not want to live in a world where the wonderful people I know, and me, are attacked, where people have to live in the closet and all the horrors that entails, where people fear to be "out" and have to mask and lie in order to survive. I don't want to go back and I guess that is one good reason that I am very happy to be out loud and proud. Everyone has something different to offer in the activism stakes. I think my next step in terms of my identity is to work out what I can do best to help keep and expand on the gains the trans and gender-diverse and autistic communities have made.

I will finish with an example of something my coming out has made possible. I was traveling for a conference recently and stayed with a friend who has two autistic children, one of whom uses they/them pronouns. This child is 11 years old. My friend said to her child, "Yenn uses they/them pronouns too." I saw the kid's face just light up. Shortly afterwards I got an (apparently rare) hug from them. As far as I am concerned, that is one of the best of all the good outcomes of my coming out. For a young child to feel accepted and respected and valued and to know adults who they have something in common with is an outcome I love. If I can help any kids and young people avoid all the misery I had to go through in my younger years—as an autistic and a non-binary person—that makes everything I do worthwhile.

---

*Yenn Purkis is a non-binary autistic advocate and author who lives in Australia with their little black kitty and wants to change the world.*

# A Letter to My Parents

**Reflections of a Trans Autistic Enby**

*Qwyrdo (they/them/their or ze/zer/zers)*

(Content notice: bullying, genitalia, death.)

Dear Mom and Dad,

This is going to be hard to read. I love you—remember that. And remember these words are written with that love in my heart, even though they probably will hurt you.

I love you, but I really wish you'd had a clue. You tried—stars know you tried—but the honest truth is, in many ways, you failed.

Do you remember when I first started speaking—not just words here or there, but full and well-structured sentences? I was about six months old. Do you remember me asking, as we drove on one of our many little trips around town, "Mommy, what's a 'mottle'?" We had just passed a sign that read M-O-T-E-L.

Do you remember the test you devised for me afterward? You showed me a stop sign and asked, "What is this?" I answered, "A stop sign." You showed me a red octagon and asked, "What is this?" I answered, "A red octagon." You showed me the letters S T O P and asked, "What is this?" And I answered, "That reads 'stop.' S-T-O-P, stop!" I was 18 months old.

Did it ever occur to you I might not be neurotypical—that my brain might work in a different way from most, that I might be autistic?

Do you remember when I first put on Mom's lipstick? When I first put on her wigs and clip-on earrings and tried to wear her clothes, which were much, much too big for me? I was about three.

Did it ever occur to you that I might not be your little boy?

Do you remember my obsessions with butterflies and sailing ships and clocks and trains? Do you remember my siblings teaching me how to say, "E equals MC squared?" Do you remember how I used to shake my head from side to side right before I went to sleep at night? I was about three.

Did it ever occur to you that I might be autistic?

Do you remember when I told you, "I was an old lady in ancient China"? Do you remember how I described dying and being transferred to your womb? I was about three.

Did it ever occur to you that I might not be your little boy?

Do you remember me asking you what the thing between my legs was? You said, "It's a penis. Boys have one. Girls have a vagina." I was about five.

Did it ever occur to you that I might not be your little boy?

Did it ever occur to you that I might take your word at face value and not question it, because I was autistic?

I was your child, but I was never your "little boy." I was always different from the other kids at school. I never had more than three or four friends. I was always autistic, only this never occurred to you.

You did know I didn't fit in. You remember, I'm sure, when I went on strike from school for a week because I was constantly bullied. I was about ten.

You did know I pursued my special interests with a keen passion. You fostered one of them—playing harpsichord—by enrolling me in lessons. You were there at the school talent show when I couldn't read the piece I'd practiced and started playing another. I was 16.

But did you know that the school's theater teacher thought I was an idiot savant—until he found out I was an International Baccalaureate student and candidate for class valedictorian? I was 18.

You did know that, in college, my world came crashing down around me. First, suicidal depression. Then, realizing I was transgender. Then, the school not accommodating my bathroom needs. I was 23.

But you didn't "see it." You didn't "see it" because I had been interested in butterflies and ships and clocks and trains as a child.

What you *didn't see* was my autism—my penchant for special interests, in which I could become absorbed for endless hours. What you *didn't see* was that I was bullied because I didn't understand, and couldn't adapt to, the social norms of my peers. What you *didn't see* was that my first taste memory was Mom's lipstick, which I had put on myself.

Maybe you saw how much I struggled trying to socially transition in my 20s. But even I didn't understand *why*. I had no idea I was autistic. I had no idea I was non-binary. I grew up being told I was a boy; that there were boys and girls; and, since I clearly was not a boy, I *must* be a girl.

I was wrong. And it took me another 15 years to figure that out.

Non-binary. That's a word—a concept—I wish you had known when I was five and asking questions. Or genderqueer. Or gender nonconforming. I can hardly begin to imagine how my life would have unfolded had I simply known there were people who were neither boys nor girls, had I known there were people not defined by what's between their legs.

Autistic. That's a word—a concept—I wish you had known when I was ten and striking from school. I can hardly begin to imagine how my life would have unfolded had I—had we—known that my brain worked differently from my peers' brains.

It took me until age 39 to figure out I was autistic. One of my partners at the time was on the spectrum. As I told her, "We may not be cut from the same cloth, but we sure came off the same loom." Our brains glitched out in similar ways. We both had interests we could absorb ourselves in—shared interests in linguistics and world-building that we talked about for hours on end with each other.

I started bugging my therapist at the gender clinic. He didn't "see it"; he didn't think autism spectrum disorder (ASD) was a "good diagnostic fit." But I got him to administer some metrics. Lo and behold, I scored high on the Ritvo Autism Asperger Diagnostic Scale. He referred me to the Autism Society, whose doctors gave me an official diagnosis.

Now my gender clinic screens *all* transgender and gender nonconforming patients for ASD.

Why am I telling you all this now? You've been gone for years. I still love and miss you. I wish you could have read this letter.

But I'm sharing it with the world, just in case some parent of a young, bright, funny person sees any bit of myself in their child. Maybe that child is precocious with language like I was; maybe they're struggling, or using words *almost* but not quite right. Maybe that child doesn't make friends easily or is bullied at school for being different. Maybe that child is autistic, and that understanding could help ease their path through this world.

Maybe that child wears your lipstick or plays with toys that are considered appropriate for the "other" gender. Maybe they'll ask you what's between their legs, and their parents can tell them about boys and girls and enbies (as we non-binary folks label ourselves). Maybe that child is transgender or non-binary themselves, and *that* understanding could help ease their path through this world.

Maybe that child or young adult will read this letter and find a light shone on their unique experience.

Or maybe a therapist or social worker will read this letter, and see parallels between one of their cases and my own.

In any case, Mom and Dad, I needed to share this. I needed to get it off my chest. I needed to tell you what you didn't know about me, what you *could* have seen in me, but didn't have the framework in which to process it.

I want you to know I still love you, despite your shortcomings. You did the best you could.

Maybe it wasn't you who failed me, but the society we live in.

Love,

Qwyrdo

---

*Qwyrdo is a white, Buddhist, 46-year-old non-binary autistic person who has special interests including planetary science, world-building, music, and trans/autistic liberation.*

# I'm trans and autistic, and yes (for me), they're related

*endever\* corbin (they/them/their or xe/xem/xyr)*

My gender is autistic.

I don't mean my gender is autism, this is not a singular noun that names something I "have," this is one of the adjectives that describes my gender, because it is one of words that describes me as a whole.

I use lots of words to describe my gender. You'll get the whole list. But if I get one word, if the world expects a summary, then I say "I am trans." I am. I don't think there is, but if there were a scale of transness from 0 to 100 percent, I figure I'd be around 117 percent. So as a summary word, it works. If I get one more word, if someone wants to pin me down into something more specific, I'll go with non-binary. Not a man or a woman. But wow, it is more complicated than that. I want you to understand why, for me, being trans is intertwined with being autistic.

My gender does not fit into normative social expectations associated with womanhood and manhood—just like my neurotype doesn't fit into normative social expectations in general. I'm pretty sure I don't even understand what those social norms are. I tried to make a spreadsheet once, to collect stereotypical traits and phenomena associated with binary genders, in order to try to correlate my own parallel traits and see if I could match up my experiences anywhere. For example, I made a category for clothes, listing quintessentially binary-coded clothes items like lingerie, pantyhose, neckties, suits, and so on. What clothes items would people who know me consider quintessential endever*? Well, probably knee socks with cool designs (birds, rainbows, dinosaurs, books, stripes) and Harry Potter t-shirts. (The socks are partly a sensory thing, and Harry Potter is my special interest, which leads us back to...hi, yes, autistic.) These are not exactly very gendery pieces of clothing. And I don't even know how lingerie or business suits work. Like—sizes, fastenings, names of components...? I never learned any of that. Nor did I learn the other allistic things people drape themselves in, expecting me to understand—facial expressions, non-verbal language. I mean, for all I know there are even differences in those minutiae between typical binary gender expressions. Maybe I can have a row on my spreadsheet for quintessentially binary-coded body language, and then, the column for my own would be filled by...what, stimming? I mean, I imagine that's the way I move which stands out to any given person around me.

So yeah, my gender is autistic. I mean, hell, do neurotypical cis people even make spreadsheets to try to figure out what gender is?

I want to explain the other words I use for my gender, less common than trans and non-binary. You may think they are absurd, too specific, meaningless trends. I do not care. I do not need your approval to be who I am.

Neurogenders are genders specific to neurodivergent people whose experience of gender relates to their neurotype or who feel they can't fully understand gender due to their neurotype. So, one of the words I use to describe my gender is neuro-enby (enby is short for non-binary).

That starts to address what I've described above. Really, the social norms of gender are endlessly mystifying to me. I can look at a group of men interacting or a group of women interacting and feel like...I don't know, another species? Or maybe like a stranger visiting a foreign land and deep in culture shock? These metaphors are too cliché to be fully accurate. I just know with my whole being that these are not my people. I do not belong. I watch, but I have no idea what's going on or why. They all seem to be using an invisible dialect that runs under, over, and alongside their spoken English, and I know that if I were to approach them and try to join the conversation I would be the odd one out, even if I'm not using augmentative and alternative communication (AAC) that day. Maybe they'd assume I was a cis person of the "opposite" binary gender; maybe they'd figure I was a gender nonconforming "one of them"; or maybe they'd manage to realize I'm trans but then would spend the entire conversation staring at me hoping for some clue as to "which direction" I've transitioned in...; or, maybe they'd just attribute my weird gender cues to a more general weirdness they might describe as outcast, crazy, eccentric, unpleasant. I mean, I can put in effort to try to "pass" as cis and neurotypical—I can try to mask my autistic traits and aim my gender expression in one direction or another—but it's really up to them whether any of it will work. Their preconceived notions about what makes a man and what makes a woman and what makes a normal brain will filter everything about me into their personal diagnostic framework and their personal gender categories.

That's often safer for me, to shift my behavior whatever way I can to try to blend into the crowd. But the thing is, it doesn't always work. Maybe I'm masking and gendering as hard as I can and they still spot the fake. Because for me being a neuro-enby means I never quite get the joke. It's not just that I feel like I'm not one of them; often they notice something about me that confirms it. People say there are five love languages or something—well, if there are two binary gender languages, I don't understand either. If there is one allistic language, I usually need a translator. So: neuro-enby. I don't understand allistic or binary genders, and probably never will. They are unfathomable, incomprehensible. Social constructs? Sure. But I've never been that good at social stuff.

Okay, so you've got some of my gender words now. The others are neutrois stargender/dryagender/fasciboy-flux contrabinary genderpunk.

Neutrois—neutral gender or lack of gender—gets closest to describing my relationship to my body. To be frank, that relationship consists mostly of distress: a dysphoria I experience first and foremost proprioceptively, perhaps due to the autistic way I process sensory information. Various medical interventions can ameliorate my dysphoria, get me closer to the body I feel would represent my internal sense of self better, but with that I have to be careful. If the provider finds out I'm autistic, will they decide I can't really be trans? I try to avoid using AAC when interacting with surgeons, out of worry they'll think I'm not competent to give consent. But...why should I have to hide who I am in order to express who I am? I am neutrois. My body feels wrong internally. Body parts are not occupying the correct airspace, nerves go in the wrong directions, when I move, my center of balance feels off. This is as integral to my sensory reality as is my difficulty processing auditory information and my hypersensitivity to bright sunlight.

Stargender: there have been stars in all of my names. My first tattoos were stars; I have always felt a strong connection to the symbol as well as the actual points of light in the sky. The way words are visually and kinaesthetically spelled is more important to me than their pronunciation, due to my autistic relationship to language and speech—so yeah, my name does have a star at the end as a silent letter. That's just how you spell it, the same way it's all lowercase because that's just how you spell it. That's what looks right. Is it autistic to be so attached to a simple abstract symbol? I don't know. But starness is more a part of me than maleness or femaleness could ever be. Plus, one of the meanings, beyond simply being the gender of a star, is that stargender refers to a gender which is unknowable. So, back to me and neurogenders.

Dryagender is a gender that has to do with the feeling of an empty forest. I was born in the forest, at least in the sense that is important. I am a creature of the forest; no matter how long I live in the city, that cannot be separated from me, just like being autistic cannot be separated from me despite how long I spent surrounded by people training me to pretend otherwise.

Fascigenders are genders specific to autistic people that relate to a special interest. Well, as mentioned, Harry Potter is my special interest. I identify as who Harry would be if he were a Ravenclaw (that is, I don't have the same personality as him, just a relatable plotline). And I swear to the gods, dying my hair black and putting on my round prescription glasses and donning robes and, wand holster feels less like drag than anything else I can think of. That's the thing—for me being neutrois means that *everything* feels like drag. My personal six-word memoir is mostly "one long drag show: no tips." But dressed as Harry, with maybe a striped Ravenclaw tie thrown in? That's better. That's maybe a little closer to me. Because my special interests are one way I express who I am. This degree of focus and enthusiasm is one of my autistic traits. I read and reread and watch and rewatch canon, I listen almost exclusively to wizard rock (fan-produced Harry Potter themed music), I collect way too much merch, I read translations of the books in Latin, Scots dialect, and other languages I want to learn, I work wizards into my school projects, I go to conventions... Harry Potter is a deep part of me. Fasciboy fits.

Flux, attached to those last three descriptors of my gender, indicates that their intensity can vary over time. As far as I can tell I'm often at least a tiny bit stargender, a tiny bit dryagender, and a tiny bit fasciboy, but at some times might not be all of them at once. And the amounts can be more than just a tiny bit; the amounts and proportions vary over time. I don't bother noticing from day to day how much of each I am, I'm just so accustomed to fluctuations I don't take note of them unless I consciously consider it. Maybe this could relate to alexithymia and problems with interoception and other autistic differences in reading internal states, or maybe it's just not important to me to narrow down. I don't know.

Okay, now the juicy ones are left, which is that I'm a contrabinary genderpunk. I made up, to the best of my knowledge, the adjective contrabinary, but genderpunk has been around for a while. Contrabinary means my gender is in direct opposition to the gender binary system—it's not just that it doesn't fit comfortably within that system, it's that it actively defies it. My contrabinary gender exists as a proclamation of war. (Okay, I've got nothing against non-cissexist people who personally identify as a single binary gender, it's the construct and the violence implicit to it that are the problem.) And for me, genderpunk, which I use as more of a noun, represents some of the style and politics of resistance I associate with my gender. It's a word I endeavor to embody the way I endeavor to embody "autpunk." That is: screw the cops, stim with pride, down with cis, eat the rich, defiance not compliance, binders and glitter, spikes and patches, chew necklaces and wearable AAC. I will fuck up your normal with my autistic brain and my trans body and my special interest clothes and the way I move and the way I communicate and my scribbles over your check-one-box paperwork and my anti-cure response to your medical model—and yeah, the way I spell my name.

My gender is autistic. Maybe a month from now or a year from now or a decade from now I'll have found a different set of words to feel like home in, but for now this collection describes how these aspects of who I am define each other.

If you know someone else who is neurogender, or another gender you've never heard of, or simply autistic plus trans of any kind, believe them when they tell you who they are. *Tell* them you believe them. And then tell the world that you believe us, and so should everyone.

---

*endever\* is a mentally ill queer Ravenclaw who writes, makes wizard rock, and does crafts. Xe is synaesthetic, somewhat faceblind, semi-verbal, and uses AAC part time.*

# Evolving H

H A Clark (xe/xem/xyr or they/them/their)

I am autistic. I am non-binary.

I was diagnosed with Asperger's syndrome at six years old. There was some history of autism on my father's side of the family: one of his cousins is autistic. I was able to communicate. I had a big imagination. I was clever. I had friends. In many ways, I fit more into the "female-coded autism" models than traditional "male-coded" autism. This is still something I struggle with.

Back then, it was just words to me. I didn't know what it meant. Who cares?

I mostly lived in my own imaginary world. I became obsessed with things. I got along better with cats than humans. I wanted to be a cat. When I dug my heels in about something I could be very stubborn. I had trouble reading people. I spent a lot of time reading books.

My mother sometimes tells the story of how she'd been talking about something related to another person and I piped up with, "Who cares? They're not real people." After some digging, it turned out I believed that me and her were the only real people and everyone else was some kind of robot. The reason for her exception was based in the fact that she sometimes said, "I think..."

I wanted to grow a beard. I wanted to run around topless. I hated skirts. I hated pink. That stuff's just being a tomboy, right?

I grew up, and as I came to understand autism more my relationship with it became more complicated. I was bothered by comparisons to more "typical" portrayals of autism and would wonder if I was faking it. It took a long time to come to terms with how autism was inextricably a part of my identity without being all of who I was.

During my teenage years, I would sometimes lay awake at night imagining I had a penis, reaching down and finding nothing there. I became disgusted with myself, told myself these thoughts were sick, wrong, evil, and I should bury them away. Besides, I also wanted breasts, so it must be nothing, right?

During my GCSEs, one of the subjects I did was psychology. We looked at Freudian theories of development during one of the modules. I looked at it and went, "See? It's perfectly normal for girls to dream of having penises. Granted, you should have grown out of it by now, but that can probably be attributed to autism causing developmental delays."

The unit also made a distinction between "sex" as physical traits and "gender" as psychological traits, but I didn't think too deeply on it.

My first real exposure to transgender issues was when a good friend came out, originally as genderfluid but later as non-binary and most recently as a non-binary trans man. I contextualized it in my brain, back then, using the sex/gender distinction mentioned in my psychology lessons. The model has its flaws, but it was an important stepping stone for me.

As I looked into it a bit more, I began to grow more interested because to some part of me the idea of not having to be a girl because of my body resonated with it. Another part of my brain slammed down on those thoughts: "Do you want to give people another reason to label you as weird? Do you want to be persecuted? Look at all these stories of things trans people go through. You're just being stupid and thinking about jumping on a bandwagon with no regard for the consequences." So I shoved the thoughts back into a box and buried them, although I did still retain a certain interest in the topic.

Throughout my childhood I had long hair, but when I turned 18

I decided to make a change and get a pixie cut. I went to university to study physics, living at home because my autistic ass couldn't survive by myself. The hour-and-a-half commute was hell but it was better than the alternative. I was going to be a theoretical physicist when I grew up.

With my hair short, people increasingly started to clock me as male instead of female. At first it bothered me and I got stressed about it. But as time passed, within a year I noticed myself getting ready in the morning aiming for an androgynous look, and wondering how many people would call me "he" today.

I began to struggle badly at university. There were accommodations made for my autistic self, and I had regular contact with the disability department via their mentoring program, but it wasn't enough. I had always been an academic high achiever, and had hung most of my self-esteem on that pillar, so starting to fail hit my self-esteem badly. I was diagnosed with depression and general anxiety disorder, and began to see a cognitive behavioral therapist.

Meanwhile, I reopened the box of questioning my gender. After some weeks thinking about it, I got in touch with my friend mentioned earlier and had a conversation about it. A couple of weeks later, I came out to my mother as non-binary. I am extremely lucky because I have a very supportive mother, whether about my autism, my gender, and whatever else, but I won't pretend that it wasn't nerve-wracking for me.

My experience with learning how my autism fits with my identity was useful here, because it provided me with a framework for understanding how my gender identity fits in as well.

I barely scraped through my first year at university. The first course of therapy lasted for six weeks before I was discharged. As my second year moved forward, however, my grades continued to drop and my mental health plummeted. After talking to my mother about it, I got in touch with my former therapist again about the fact I was feeling suicidal.

I was referred to another therapist for a more intensive, 12-week course of cognitive behavioral therapy. Meanwhile, I began to come out to more people. The therapist was supportive when I came out in the context of a discussion about something that had upset me, for which I used an example of people misgendering me repeatedly after I had already come out to them.

However, with the threat of exams looming, my mental health continued to decline. By the end of the spring term, I was feeling seriously suicidal practically every day and didn't trust myself to be alone. The day before my first exam, I snapped and had to send a message to the department head saying I was having a mental breakdown and couldn't do this.

I visited the GP, obtained a letter of evidence for the university about my mental breakdown, and was put on antidepressants. I was allowed to defer my exams until September.

I spent the summer taking things one day at a time. I took my deferred exams that September but didn't pass the year. I could have looked at options to retake the year but, with my mental health a total wreck, I dropped out instead.

In the two years since then, my mental health has improved but I don't think I'll ever be truly better. I have learned a lot more about autism, gender, and my relationship with both in that time. I can't ever go back to what I was before.

H survived and came through the other side of the breakdown. Heather didn't.

---

*H is an autistic enby with a special interest in cats, and formerly also physics. Xe enjoys reading (mainly fantasy/science fiction), the outdoors, and Dungeons and Dragons.*

# The Power of Perspective

*Megan Talbot (she/her/hers)*

I have never lived in one place for very long. My dad worked for an oil company, which meant that we moved fairly frequently. I remember reading so many of my report cards from various schools in which the phrase "seems to be settling in well" was a common refrain. When I was 13, I read this once again in a report from my latest school, in Russia. I don't know if it was because I had finally grown tired of moving so often or if it was some fit of teenage bloody-mindedness, but at that moment I resolved that I would never see those words on a report card again. I would not settle in. I would not allow myself to be changed for the convenience of others. Places would have to adapt to me, I would no longer allow myself to conveniently "fit in." To this day, I cannot tell if this was teenage me being singularly stupid or unusually wise. I think it may well have been both.

School in Russia did not go well. I was always a particularly awkward child, and this didn't get better with age. To a degree, I suppose my resolution to not change myself to fit in may have been moot, as I'm not sure I could have even if I had tried. For various reasons, it was decided that I would benefit from some stability, so, largely because my dad's company would pay for it, an attempt was made to send me to boarding school. The school in question required new applicants to undergo not only testing to evaluate their academic abilities, but also an interview with the headmaster, and to submit an educational psychologist report. It was because of this process that it was first identified that I had Asperger's syndrome (which would now have been diagnosed as autism spectrum disorder), although this would not be confirmed until I was 17. I never did get into that school, in large part because it was decided that it was not the place for me after I was asked about my attitude towards a school which served no apparent purpose other than to uphold tradition (the school in question had a rich history and many inexplicable traditions).

There was no real follow-up to the suggestion that I may have had autism spectrum disorder, and I moved to Texas, for the second time, where I again experienced educational problems, mostly relating to getting on with others and arguing with teachers. After a singularly unhappy period in which it was established that, despite it being the popular diagnosis at the time, I did not have attention deficit hyperactivity disorder (ADHD) and the medication for it did me no good whatsoever, it was decided that whatever was wrong with me it was probably best not to label me. As such, my experiences with psychologists and psychiatrists focused on attempting to help me cope with life rather than trying to find a specific name or diagnosis for my problem. One psychologist in particular decided that the root of my issues was that I was insufficiently masculine, and so a lot of effort was spent encouraging me to play rugby and other games that I was particularly bad at and did not enjoy.

Whatever resolution my parents had made that I should not be labeled evaporated by the time I was 17. I had finally got in to a boarding school to do my A-levels in the UK, but I was singularly unhappy. My glasses were being broken regularly due to persistent bullying, but I was as strange and unpleasant as ever. Eventually I was sent away after the school decided they could not fulfill the duty of care that they owed me as a boarder—not due to the unceasing bullying, but because I attempted suicide. I am not going to go into details about that as it would help no one and be unpleasant to write and probably more so to read. Following this, I had a period away from school while we waited for an NHS psychiatrist to see me and produce a report for the school. The appointment itself was anti-climactic considering the two-month wait for it. It lasted 40 minutes and on hearing that it had been suggested that I may have Asperger's syndrome the psychiatrist set about confirming the diagnosis by asking various questions, and by the end of the appointment he was satisfied that I did in fact have Asperger's and he produced a report for the school to that effect. The school then allowed me to return as a boarder, which I never understood. If their concern was that they could not meet my needs, I don't see how that diagnosis made my needs evaporate, as no additional resources were made available. It was at the school that I first said aloud to a friend that I wished that I had been born a girl. She asked if I had considered a "sex change," and I dismissed it, largely because it had never occurred to me that it was an option. That dismissal did not last long, and I came out as trans three months later, two months after leaving that school due to the persistent bullying.

I am now, despite not being even vaguely intelligent, a lecturer in law at a university in Wales. I have an LLB in law, as well as an LLM (a bachelor's and master's degree respectively) and will soon, god willing, have a PhD. I teach a number of legal topics, particularly contract law, family law and medical law, and my research focuses on the legal recognition of non-binary gender identities. I have been transitioned and on hormones for ten years now. I have achieved what I suppose by some metrics may be considered a measure of success, particularly considering the bleak moments during my teenage years. As such, while I am by no means at the pinnacle of success, I thought I would share the things to which I attribute what measure of success I have had, despite the misery they caused me as a teenager, and I hope make some wider points about diversity and the power that our differences can gift us.

I have, at times, cursed various aspects of my identity. I have cursed my transness for making me visibly physically different from others, or marking me as a target for bigotry, for giving me a voice that I hate with every fibre of my being. I have cursed my autism spectrum disorder for making interacting with others so difficult, for rendering me essentially deaf to so much non-verbal or non-overt communication, for making me at times feel so alien from other people that I felt that I was simply incompatible with existence. I would be lying if I said this had ever totally gone away. I still accidentally upset my friends, although I am getting better at that, but it's a difficult learning experience, as I hate causing bother or upset to others. I still have gender dysphoria, and still from time to time lose an entire day to being misgendered and feeling so utterly drained that I am unable to make progress on my work.

However, I tend now to view my transness and autism spectrum disorder less as problems that I must suffer with and simply differences that can, in many way, be assets. I am very fortunate that I am able to teach and research law, which is one of my special interests. As a result, my work often does not feel like work, but something I do for fun that the university has decided to pay me for, which I think is one of the best situations a person can be in. I still have problems with many things that people consider to be trivial parts of everyday life. For example, I wear headphones whenever I leave the house to combat anxiety and occasionally to protect myself from overwhelming crowd or traffic noise. I also have problems talking to people I don't know or dealing with unexpected changes, problems which the somewhat flexible nature of academic work allow me to compensate for. However, these problems lead me to view my brain as specialized, rather than broken in some fundamental way. My life would be significantly bleaker if I had not been able to enter academia or found how much I loved law. Our society has a tendency to undervalue love—not love in the romantic sense, which may well be overvalued, but love of things, passion for subjects or activities that bring you profound joy. We tend to think in terms of skill, talent, abilities, and aptitudes, but I contend that love of a subject is a talent in its own regard.

If you ever find yourself having grim thoughts that your brain is broken or that you are incompatible with existence, take a moment to think about the things you love. Your passions are not just quirks, or aspects of your personality to be set aside, they are a part of what makes you unique and a significant asset. A person who does not love a thing will likely never be sufficiently motivated to invest the time in something to become an expert in it. Similarly, time you spend on your passions will often not feel like work to you, even though it may to someone who does not share your love of the subject at hand. That ability, to derive joy and even energy from something that others find taxing, should never be underestimated. You may feel talentless or useless, but with a small amount of effort or assistance the things you love can allow you to surpass even renowned figures in your field.

One of the most interesting aspects of my transness and autism spectrum disorder is how they have altered my metaphorical position in the world. What I mean by this is simply that the things I experience are different due to these aspects of my identity. If I were not trans I would most likely be less aware of the avalanche of transphobia currently being spewed in our national press, for example. These experiences necessarily impact what I am aware of and how I perceive the world. If I were not trans I would have the luxury of paying less attention to transphobia, or underestimating its severity. Similarly, if I did not have autism spectrum disorder I would no doubt be less acutely aware of how various institutional practices negatively impact people with disabilities. While this perspective is granted in part by having to deal with unpleasant things, I tend to view it as an asset. The insight granted to me by this perspective has assisted me greatly, as I see problems that others may overlook or underestimate, and I have the drive to fix them. To date I have been fairly successful. My university has already altered a number of its practices that led to the inadvertent outing of trans students and staff, and I have, with assistance, started a group to help support trans students. I have written ethical guidance for those researching gender, helped improve trans access to sport, and written my university's guidance for managers with regards to the treatment of trans employees. This is why I started this essay writing about my refusal to "settle in" to institutions. While this arguably did not serve me well as a teenager, as I have gotten older it is one of the aspects of my personality I have become most thankful for. As I have grown my knowledge and expertise and demonstrated this to others, my insistence that institutions adapt has transformed from something that caused me a great deal of strife to a powerful driver for change.

My attitude is not exactly the same as it was when I was younger. Whereas then it was somewhat a selfish and egotistical refusal to change, it has since evolved and adopted more philosophical sophistication. My current stance is that people in disadvantaged groups should not be asked to change themselves or be exposed to harm simply so that society does not have to change. Institutions are, due to their size and resources, vastly more able to change, for example to become less hostile to people with disabilities, than a disabled person is to become less disabled. Unfortunately, because institutions are mostly run by those who are in a majority they often cater to the needs of the majority far better than they cater to the needs of anyone else. This leads to a situation where those who are hurt by the institution must advocate for their own interests in an attempt to change the institution, despite being already in a position where they are less able to do this. As such, much of my work at the moment is devoted to supporting others less able to advocate for their own interests, and to ensuring that the institution devotes resources to self-correction. The hope is that this will lead to the institution shouldering the burden for its own improvement, rather than this falling to individuals who are already experiencing hardship due to institutional flaws.

Of course, this sort of activism is not for everyone. While I am happy that I am in a position to be able to advocate for change, I know that not everyone has the ability or desire to do the same. Furthermore, it is not reasonable to assume that everyone who is disadvantaged due to disability or discrimination should have to be an activist to protect themselves from institutional structures that cause them harm. This assumption is one that many institutions make, that if someone has a problem they will be able to advocate for change in a way that is both effective and approved of by the institution, which can be challenging in and of itself. Many institutions are designed in such a way that means their structures are very resistant to change, particularly if the need for change is not couched in terms that they value, such as economic gain. Because not everyone can be an activist, nor should they be expected to be, and institutions can be change resistant, which can be draining on anyone who does attempt activism, it is important for institutions and the individuals who have power within them to be introspective. This enables change without placing the burden on individuals least able to bear it. However, when looking at the world around them, people often fall for a number of psychological traps that lead them to fail to identify possible changes and how they can be implemented.

One of the most pernicious psychological pitfalls I have noticed is the power of the norm. People tend to approach their day-to-day lives making a number of assumptions about the world. In particular, most people assume that most people are more or less the same as they are. On the one hand, this can be a positive. Assuming that people are more or less like you may make empathizing with them easier, and it may be the case that it would be overwhelming to constantly be aware of the unique complexity of every individual. On the other hand, this assumption can often make things harder when someone's experience significantly differs from our own. For example, this assumption can lead a person to assume that things that they find harmless are harmless to everyone. As a result of this there can often be a lack of consideration for people who find certain things, such as being in louder environments, more difficult. Not only can this lead to people not noticing when they are inadvertently making things more difficult for people who don't share their characteristics, but it has a more insidious side effect of entrenching the perceived "normal" status quo. This is because if you assume that everyone has a similar experience to yours you tend to think of actions that suit you as suiting everyone.

A prime example of the problem of the norm comes from when I was doing my course for teaching in higher education. I found the course particularly alienating, because it was quite clear that their model of a good teacher was a neurotypical teacher. A great deal of time was devoted to presentation skills, and how one shouldn't stammer and should make eye contact but not too much eye contact. I was disturbed by how much good teaching was defined as the absence of bad teaching, and that bad teaching was always identified as being caused by certain actions or a lack of actions that correlated with various disabilities. For example, we were told that a good teacher should move around the class to "own the space" and ensure everyone was engaged. When I asked if that meant the teaching of a person with mobility problems was going to necessarily be worse for lacking this aspect of good teaching, I was simply told "obviously you work with what you have." When I mentioned how alienated I had felt as a result of how much of what I was told good teaching was were things I have a great deal of difficulty with (such as eye contact), I was simply told that "obviously you can't cater for everyone, and we have to cater to the majority."

This is something I encounter fairly frequently, that the reason for a lack of inclusiveness is because the majority must always be catered for. The problem is that when this explanation is used it is often not always fully considered, because invariably in such situations, the majority is not actually being catered for as well as they could be. This is because people tend to assume that people's experiences are similar to theirs, so if they are experiencing no problems, there are no problems. However, success is not simply the absence of problems. In the case of the teaching course, while there was no problem evident to the organizer, the majority was still missing out on valuable insights into how to cater to students with different capabilities. Often fixing the problems identified by people who are impacted by the shortcomings of the status quo benefits everyone, but these benefits were invisible to the majority because it simply didn't come to their attention that there was a shortcoming or possible benefit. This is readily evident in teaching, when changes designed to assist people with specific learning difficulties actually benefit all students, but they are sometimes not implemented because teachers take an "if it ain't broke, don't fix it" approach, and are unable to see that it is in fact broken due to their perspective and lack of personal experience of the problems that do exist.

Because of this, despite the difficulties I encounter, I am often glad that my identity and experiences sometimes place me outside the norm. As much as they can sometimes make life more difficult, particularly when it comes to discrimination, I think my unique placement in the world and my experiences have also given me a number of tools for doing good in the world.

I am under no illusion that I am in any way special. What success I have achieved is not particularly remarkable. However, we live in a world where people are often systemically told that they cannot succeed, and where they are denied the assistance they need to get over small hurdles that prevent them from achieving excellence. As such, while I doubt that what I have written is particularly profound or life-changing, I hope it has served as a somewhat personal illustration of a few key points: that difficulty in certain areas is not the same as being broken; that diversity is a strength that enables us to identify problems that may otherwise go ignored, and to solve them, which benefits everyone; that institutions should shoulder the burden for their own improvement, and should actively seek out improvement rather than asking those they hurt to fix the problem themselves. And perhaps that, when it comes to achieving positive change, a certain kind of stubborn bloody-mindedness is not always a bad thing.

---

*Megan Talbot is an autistic trans woman living in Wales where she teaches law at the University of Aberystwyth and researches legal gender recognition.*

# Half a Century of Winging It

*Heather Rowan Nichol (they/them/theirs)*

I was born in the early 1960s. At that time, in the English-speaking world, the papers of Hans Asperger were unknown. The major source of knowledge was the work of Leo Kanner, covering the more severe presentations that in time became known as "classic autism." I wonder how differently things might have turned out had I been born 24 years later.

The obsessive features were there from the start. I would become so engrossed in a toy such as Lego that my mum would chase me around with a sandwich to ensure I ate something. Language seemed to follow a distinctive pattern. None of the usual babbles and bits. Nothing, and then complete sentences. The systematizing interests were there as well. "Why?" "How does it work?" "Say what it does?" were the questions asked.

The age of three gave what I can now see as a big hint that things were a bit rocky with the social instinct. The opportunity arose for my mother to return to teaching, one day a week covering maternity leave at a school that had a nursery class. What a splendid opportunity for both of us: my mum to return to a profession of which she was fond and me to start with a bigger social setting than just the one or two other young ones in my parents' social circle.

Sadly, no. I hated the nursery class, and there were tears every week on nursery day. I did not get the idea of fitting in with others. I heard the feedback many years down the line that I would march

101

round the opposite way to everyone else when we did the "music and movement" classes common at the time, and I seemed to prefer having my attention on a book rather than other children. My journal noted many years after that, "Poor Mrs. Bryce, who took the class, did not deserve that year of hard work." I understand that later she spoke of having read about children like that, but never expected to teach one.

Primary school was interesting. In the first year, reception class was hard going. I seemed to keep having incidents where I would get something wrong in the social department, and then get so anxious about it an asthma episode would result. They were a feature of my primary school years. I am sure now they were anxiety triggered, and I was grateful that as my schooling went on they became less severe and less frequent, and were gone by the time I started secondary school.

Year two was one I recall being stress free, and one where I was getting on with work—reading, writing, and doing sums. My year three teacher had told my mum early on that she wished she and I could have made a visit together to the museum, as I would probably have learned more in an afternoon than she could have taught in a term. Year three was interrupted by a house move to a different city following re-organizations in my father's work.

Now in those first two years at primary school someone had spotted that something was not usual in my social or learning profile. I know this because one morning instead of walking to school we drove to a single-storey building a bit like school or a health center, and I was asked to try various little exercises—I recall one with colored wood blocks of different lengths, like those we used in class as one of the many means to help "get the idea" of numbers and arithmetic. I also recall there was a camera on the desk, without film, and my attention was taken completely by the small circular patch of light that flashed on when the shutter button was pressed. I learned many years later that it had been a visit to the shrink, which had not been especially conclusive—some conjecture being offered that perhaps neither brain hemisphere was dominant and this might be behind some of the oddities, but that one should not worry unduly.

I suspect 25 years later the conclusion would have been different, as by that time autism was understood as a much broader spectrum thanks to the research of Lorna Wing and Judith Gould, and the shrink may have put an actual label on what was observed: Asperger's syndrome.

However, such understanding was many years ahead of that assessment in 1968 and instead we muddled on and winged it. My first primary school in the new home was not a total success; the head did not fully understand my needs and I was left to my own devices a lot, which meant while I absorbed a lot of unstructured information from the copies of Newnes Pictorial Knowledge in the third-year infant class, I did not get the formal stuff gripped that would open the doors to a secondary education that would fit my profile. I suspect there was a lot of advocating by my parents to which I was not privy, which in the end resulted in a change to a small voluntary-aided primary school. This school managed to keep me focused on the formal path to the point I caught up those two years, and in the end passed the entrance requirements to secondary education with a strong academic bias where I did well.

I seem to recall that the school and my profile were a good enough match for me to keep out of trouble most of the time. Handwriting was always a vexed problem, as occasionally was staying organized. Open-ended tasks, such as the weekly homework essay, were a trial, while tasks focused on an answer that was right or wrong, such as translation to or from Latin, or French, or exercises in maths, chemistry, music, or physics, were much less problematic.

As I look back on my education, I realize that I dodged an awful lot of social stuff. That last primary school was a bit of a cramming establishment, the secondary education was single sex, and with homework each night there was not a lot of time for socializing. In fact, I much preferred my own company, toys, and spaces—a spare room in which my brother and I built a fair representation of British Rail as it was at the time, and my own room in which various electronic items got built and that occasionally worked as well.

The restricted interests part of the diagnostic criteria was certainly there. "He is obsessive" was a family catch phrase, as I found out all I could about TV aerials, and then how radios and TV receivers worked, and other bits of electronics; various home-built systems started to control the model railway rather than things bought off the shelf. Not many 15-year-olds could draw a TV receiver circuit, and while a few of us had our own tellies, I suspect I was the only one of my peers whose telly was the innards of an old receiver that I had repaired and maintained. I once earned a bit of pocket money repairing the TV set next door. The family TV set was always rented so I never managed to practice fixing that.

The bicycle and riding became a growing passion, which took off in second and third year at university, to the point that I actually rode home from university at the end of my second year. Long (often solo) cycle trips were a consistent fixture of most of my adult life. My ideal holiday is still one for just me, my bicycle, my Youth Hostel Association card, a tent, and maps.

I recall well-meant advice from my mother early in my adult life that I should rein in my cycling passion and principled stance against owning my own car or I might not be able to find someone with whom to share my life. However, those long times alone in the saddle restored me, and I was not going to give them up.

The social blind spots in the profile caught up with me in the workplace, though. I was recruited, I am sure, because of the depth of electronic knowledge I demonstrated in interview combined with the activities I did in music and theatre sound, and I joined the staff of a large organization in 1985 as an engineer. I am sorry to record more than a few incidents and faux pas during my career. One of my annual reports read:

...is a first class engineer whose deductive skills are invaluable in the test room, but with an unfortunate tendency for these to stray into the operation area where the first priority is to maintain the service rather than finding the most elegant engineering solution, and a more pragmatic approach is needed... Social skill generally lacking, though there has been a slight improvement of late.

The blind spots in executive function bit me from time to time, and I had a few of what I now know were verbal warnings over the years. I also recall the long work days filled with chit chat and banter and then, after work, worrying that I had been an annoying, immature irritation to people with whom I worked.

I rattled around a small number of moves within my organization—a short secondment to our operation in a larger city two years in, then after 11 years I secured a promotion from trainee engineer to established engineer, which involved a move to the center of our organization, definitely a case of tears before bedtime at leaving not so much my home but the landscape that I loved passionately, and the very strong community of eccentrics with which I cycled. Another secondment two years later saw me spend two-and-a-half years away. A year after my return, I had a sideways move, being poached by another department with the offer of a fixed shift pattern—the irregular hours of my then-post having become a source of some stress.

As I look back on gender, sexuality, and relationships, I see the scientist approach coming out in me. I now realize my sexuality was strongly shaped by noticing what sort of things caused pleasant feelings in my body, as the phrase has it, "down there." Way back, almost pre-school age, and definitely around the ages of four, five, and six, dreams in which I was prisoner in a dungeon, chained up, produced a most pleasant feeling indeed. So did dreams in which I was wearing a garment of soft rubber around my waist and the top of my legs. I am afraid a very happy dream aged seven set off a terribly strong fetish association from that point onwards.

I learned of how new life was started off through the Ladybird Book *Your Body*, which described it all in neutral, matter-of-fact ways in language that was right for the age when I read it. As I moved into my teenage years, I learned I would start to fancy girls and move in the direction of girlfriends and eventually marriage, although in the "photographic" (all right, "top shelf") magazines which we clandestinely circulated, all the effort the models, wardrobe supervisors, lingerie suppliers, and photographers made turned out to be wasted as far as my mind and body went. The only issue of the magazine of choice that provided satisfying reading and viewing was the one that interviewed two cottage industry makers of bondage, sadism, dominance, and masochism (BDSM) equipment—collars, cuffs, body harnesses, and the like—and the photo shoot of their wares gave me much enjoyment but some censure from my peers, who did not understand such things.

For gender expression and identity we have to wait until my 21st year, the summer and the end-of-term fancy dress picnic with the cycling club with which I rode. My search for a costume took me into the Oxfam shop on the pedestrianized shopping street, from which I emerged with a flowery summer dress and a flowery wide-brimmed hat (which was well received by my grandmother as a birthday present later that summer). We rather scared the civilians with our costumes as we rode out to the picnic spot—one a cross between an SAS agent and a tree, another a convict, and me, a bearded lady. I won the prize and I liked the costume and how it felt. In fact, I liked it so much it became my chosen nightwear thereafter when I was not at my parental home. Once I was in my own flat (in a different city from my parental home) that dress was worn every night until it wore out. The two fancy dress parties around work in the next three years saw me finding other more feminine costumes, which also became chosen wear in the privacy of my own home. Although I would never admit it to myself, I knew from the information that had been in the student union welfare diary that I was a transvestite. With the penumbra around the word, I understand why I did not particularly want to be honest with myself about it.

The fetish and transvestite sides have been remarkably consistent through my life, alongside all those traits that go with being on the autism spectrum. Every so often the charity shop or junk shop would provide items of clothing or equipment to allow me to enjoy those sides of myself, and then periodically I would "take self in hand" and point out to myself I would not find any long-term partner if I had those habits. The items would be donated to a charity shop in the next town, or thrown into a skip at the recycling center, but of course, those desires don't go away, do they?

My unidentified autistic traits left me far more vulnerable in the area of close relationships than I knew. My steps took me into my church in my 24th year. Three years later I had taken a kind interest in a new face at church. It was not a romantic interest at all; it was an interest based on kindness, and realization that here was someone whose life had not been smooth. However, I think it quite possible the interest was perceived as romantic. I missed all the signs it might have been perceived as such, even one as blunt as divorce papers left out. I just thought it was very careless for someone to leave an important and confidential document on view just like that.

At the same time, at a workcamp holiday, I made a connection with another human being that has proved to be lifelong. A card I slipped in another's rucksack became a correspondence, a process later described by that person as a gentle "dancing circles round each other" as we corresponded. It was one of those processes that could quite likely have drawn us together as romantic partners in due course except that...

With the person in whom I had taken a kind interest at my local meeting, I discovered interesting things about eye contact one night after a shared meal. I noticed as I watched their face that it seemed to undergo all sorts of changes, looking quite different at different times. Quite fascinating. Oh dear, that same interaction must have seemed quite different from the other person's view. We ended up far closer than I had expected, with no desire for such on my part or even any thought that we would. What a high stress and tangled year *that* one was, followed by a year of grief realizing it had closed the door to the prospect of a really close and intimate relationship with someone I *did* want to have in my life, my companion and correspondent found at that workcamp holiday. A lesson learned the very hard way. My first lover and I remain friends.

The story does have a happy ending though. My companion from the workcamp holiday has been a lifelong friend, correspondent, mutual confidant, and honorary sister.

I made some discoveries on the overlap of sexuality and gender during that first sexual relationship. By convention, I should have enjoyed being on top and being enclosed but I much preferred being on the bottom. There was a hint of that aspie logic there. I knew I was the heavier person. I didn't like the feeling of being squashed, I was sure my partner liked such a feeling even less. It made so much more sense for me to be the person lying on their back. But then there came a second unbidden feeling, that I also wanted to be the one who was not only on their back but *my* legs were the ones that parted to allow another one inside my body.

The following year, I approached a counseling service, seeking help to untangle that set of circumstances. In the course of those sessions I had more hints about my autistic profile. In the second session, the counselor drew attention to how little eye contact I had made. In the course of several sessions, I had the chance to learn some new skills in the area of assertion, and find informed reading matter on the whole area of human relationships and how minds might work, which I devoured. The service derived a useful stream of income from my purchases from their bookshop.

A subsequent close relationship ran much more smoothly, not least because after first meeting, I did a whole series of questions and answers in my private journal before following up the address the other person had passed on after our first meeting. That meeting had been by chance, and was a long and information-rich yarning session in the youth hostel where our cycle journeys had intersected before going on our separate ways the following day.

Anyway, lest I bore the reader with even more details of my personal and professional history, let us fast forward to the year 2014. I was working away in my side job—a passion for electrical installation had by that time led to getting my electrician qualifications back in 2006, joining a professional body and running a little side business as an electrician. The work was going well, there was internet access and in the evening I was watching various little things on YouTube when I came across Temple Grandin's televized talk on University of California Television titled, "My Experience of Autism."

I was captivated by Dr. Grandin's style—detail after detail, information, and a sense of humor that I caught immediately. Many of her descriptions of certain parts of the autistic profile matched the jokes we engineers make at our own expense. Also, something which had seemed so mysterious at times in the past when I had heard of it no longer seemed mysterious when told in the first person. I told a few "engineer" jokes to myself and then let it subside.

On my way home I visited my honorary sister and shared the great enjoyment I had derived from that lecture. In response, she fired the question: "Are *you* autistic?" at me. I think I blustered something to the contrary in reply. After all, how could someone like me, who was outwardly successful, be autistic? Had I not recovered from some most tangled situations in close relationships over the years? Had I not been in continuous employment for nearly 30 years and survived all the re-organizations and redundancy trawls? I think not, my dear readers.

My honorary sister is a secondary school teacher with enough experience that that innocent question may have been a little "informed." She has, after all, taught classes where one or two members have been known to be on the spectrum. Two years later she most helpfully wrote a report on me for my autism assessment.

The little jokes about myself and perhaps a slight suspicion there was more to them than just jokes did not go away. Later that autumn, I was off work with a cold, a little bored and with access to the internet and so I googled Asperger's tests and found an online version of Simon Baron-Cohen's AQ50 screening tool. I filled it in for a laugh.

The result wiped the smile right off my face. On the threshold said the result. I found another screening tool. Over the threshold again, both in overall score and in three of the four areas. Another screening tool: "You have both neurotypical and neurodiverse traits."

At this point I had found a new "special interest." I did a great deal of reading and listening to first-person testimony over the next two years, also dredging through my memory and journal, filling my journal with notes. The following summer, the mother of a young lad who is on the spectrum asked me point blank, "Are you Asperger's?" though she knew nothing of my suspicions and research. That suspicion was not going to go away.

In those same years, I had started revisiting gender expressions. Cross-dressing had come and gone over the years. It had lain dormant for about a decade, then a conversation led to a nice wig being passed on to me. Then I made some impulse buys at the London Fetish Fair and the Birmingham Bizarre Bazaar. Then in Chesterfield Market, I found an ankle-length black skirt for only £6, and who can resist a bargain? Not only that, I had quickly found a presentation that worked. It was definitely feminine if the beard was shaved off. It was understated and I did not draw a great deal of attention. It was non-threatening. When I went out to the theater, the lady in the next seat struck up a conversation and we talked about comfortable footwear. Sometimes I even got called "love" when I went out in feminine clothes. I also got plenty of "sirs" as well, so a male history can also be read.

In 2016, I attended my first Autscape. I did not have enough leave from work to do the whole conference, nor was there any residential accommodation left, but I was able to attend the registration day and first half of the first day. I found one lecture, "The Professional Autie," very informative. The speaker was a retired solicitor who had, to his considerable surprise, been diagnosed as autistic quite late in life. A professional career and an autistic profile could co-exist. In his professional life, he had made good use of the detail focus that is a feature of the autistic profile; in the end, his career had hit a limit when the social blind spots became an obstacle to the "networking" senior partners in law firms need to do to maintain and expand their client base. I joined the Wrong Planet online forums after that Autscape, read a member's account of their journey to diagnosis and some weeks later I felt a certainty that I needed to seek an informed assessment.

I did not want to go the full clinical route. I knew there were many people with very serious difficulties as adults—finding or keeping work and housing, forever landing in difficult relationships—and they had to have first claim on the resources of the NHS. For them, that clinical diagnosis might be essential to chase away a dismissal and gain reasonable adjustments, or open the doors to what statutory benefits might be available. I needed none of those, though I did want to know how accurate my own suspicions were and how good my research had been.

I had the means to pursue an assessment privately, and chose to approach a firm that did training and consultancy. I booked a non-clinical assessment against the diagnostic criteria, to take place four days after my 53rd birthday.

By now I was also having a bit of fun with gender. I didn't feel like I was in the wrong body, but I did like feminine presentations as well as masculine ones. I had already bought a utility kilt and liked it, and liked the way a lady going the other way at a big station had said, "Hey, sexy" as I walked past. I had bought more kilts the following year and these had replaced trousers as my default clothing. I enjoyed giving my best skirt outings as well, and finding that as long as I was not setting out in my own thoughts to deceive others that I had a female body, I was confident and pulled the presentation off without hassle. I chose my occasions carefully though. Pubs were out, restaurants were okay, if there was a long train journey that was good, because that is controlled space where a toilet is just a toilet. I had privilege, that of being able to choose without feeling pain and distress at the times I was not visible.

As the assessment approached I went through some periods of disquiet. Would the assessment find no evidence of my being on the spectrum? Would I leave accused of wasting the assessor's time, that I had formed a silly notion and then cherry picked a few anecdotes from my history to support it with confirmation bias? Would I leave feeling a fool and a time waster? This was one reason I had not chosen the clinical route and the NHS. Had I discovered I had wasted the resources of the NHS on some silly whim I would have felt terrible.

At last the day arrived. Payment had been made. Notes by my honorary sister and my beloved had been dispatched to the assessor. Completed autism spectrum quotient (AQ) and empathy quotient (EQ) screening tests had been returned, together with notes I had made on how I had answered or why I had given certain answers. Evenings reminiscing with my mum had been made into notes and sent on. Pages from my private journal had been typed and sent on. Twenty-five pages of notes in total, "a new record" my assessor said after the assessment.

The notes were worthwhile. "Extremely helpful" was the assessor's comment. The interview was completed in half the allocated time. "Definitely autistic, can see it a mile off" was one of the quips in the feedback afterwards. Profile definitely so, the assessment tool had picked out a spread of 15 out of a possible 18, over the threshold by two in every category, over by three in one. However, and this was marked as a considerable achievement in the report, I seemed to have used the strong points so well I had avoided that profile disabling me in the important areas of employment, housing, and relationships. It is true my present relationships are non-standard, long distance, not living under the same roof, but they are *very* low stress. I have not climbed the greasy management pole in my work, but I have been consistently employed in a role that makes use of my knowledge and skills, and kept out of trouble.

Knowing my profile is autistic has been a liberation. I feel as if I have found the pages that were missing from the technical manual. A lot of internalized shame is now gone. I also see how my fetish interests and the sensory side of the autistic profile overlap. The kit I have built gives me such positive sensory input from whole body pressure together with a sense of being in a very safe place that I will not be giving it up any time soon, and in fact I seem to be finding common ground with others in the fetish community.

An unstructured social event remains a sore trial. I still have ones where I feel as if I am that three-year-old in the nursery class, hating every minute of it. I don't like high noise levels. I did not raise it in the assessment simply because I have been able to live my life in such a way that I have avoided these situations, so I did not realize it was a feature of my profile. I was brought up with a start at my beloved's joint 50th party when I only just held it together for the evening, and towards the end I just wanted to run back to my hotel room, throw myself on the bed, and sob.

So indeed, I am a very lucky autistic old bugger indeed. Lucky, because I realized I have winged things well enough to hold down a job with good terms and conditions and a pension, and which makes good use of specialist knowledge rather than intuitive people skills. Lucky, because I have found that the place I seem to plot in the trans spectrum is one where rather than feeling a painful conflict between my sense of being masculine or feminine versus my body type, I find pleasure in and feel confident with a wide range of gender expressions, including those not conventional for the body I was born with.

I'm lucky because it happened that the areas where I found those all-encompassing passionate interests were ones I could turn into qualifications and employment, and in a field and firm where borderline autistic traits are common enough not to stand out. The work enabled me to live in my own place, meaning my delight in dressing femme at home or enjoying fetish interests would not disturb another person. I managed to extricate myself from that first demanding relationship without things falling into enmity. It occurs to me there are many like me who have not had that good fortune, and instead have spent lifetimes being told they are dirty and perverted, or they are weird, or "If you only made the effort..." A lucky old devil indeed, managing to find my various tribes and wing things so well undiagnosed.

---

*Heather Rowan Nichol is 55-year-old electrical and electronic engineer, with both a day job and a small business. Their favorite pastime is traveling alone by bicycle.*

# Five Poems

*Jan (they/them/theirs)*

## WE ARE THE STORM

We are the storm. It is nature
and nature is never wrong nor right.
We will always be part of the dances,
of the faces of humankind.

But sometimes we have to pretend:
we keep the storm safely contained.

You say you do not hate us
but you hate the cold spells
and the sweeping gales, and curse
all the rainbow-colored rain.

But if we cannot pour down
how can we wash away the haze?

You say it is just a drizzle,
only a temporary breeze.
The whirlwind and the downpour
are not there when you cannot see.

But if you only feel the draft
It is because we spare you the hurricane.

We are the storm. We are relentless
and we are here day and night.
Without announcement we take our spaces
Because we are humankind.

## THE WEIRD PEOPLE

The weird people are everywhere
You wouldn't know just by looking at them
Although you'll see there's something odd
Something not quite intense about them

They don't move or dance around
In the same way that we do
They're not as curious as we are
About beauty, love, or truth

They don't seem to understand
Our many ways to show affection
They expect everyone to act the same
We can't work out their intentions

They believe we're pretty pieces
In some puzzle that they built
We just wish that someone told them
"Thanks, but we don't want to fit!"

They're not so bad, the weird ones
They're just differently wired
Their world is dull, still, and quiet
But they can also be admired

They try to figure us out too
The most naive say some are "mild"
We may be soft, or bright, or blue
But we are nothing short of wild!

## BEAUTIFUL

If I keep saying
you are beautiful
is because nature
wrote you like a poem.

Even if others
read you differently
you possess, hidden,
your own truth.

## NON-BINARY

I exist
in the transitions;
in the gaps
between words.

I am not "partially"
something you
already know.
I am whole.

I am non-binary.
Outside the boxes.

In-between the concepts,
because I make them

outdated.
I break the models
like a storm
wreaks havoc.


## TWILIGHT

Like twilight,
we are elusive,
we are disrupting.
Like colors,
we may stand out,
we may blend in.
Like stars,
no one can bring us down.

---

*Jan is a PhD student in computer science from Argentina. They are non-binary, bisexual, and autistic. They love writing, cycling, coffee, and playing the piano.*

# What I Wish I'd Known

*Chris Breedt (they/them/their or he/him/his)*

When I sat down to write this piece it was ten days after Christmas. It's two days before the due date now and I'm tapping into my anxiety over deadlines to try to find that seam of gold that always helped me get my book assignments done the night before they were due.

I have known about the piece for months, but somehow, as with so many other things in my life, it had fallen off the back of my to-do list and got trapped in the dust bunnies under the furniture of my mind. I think at the time I had somehow feared this would happen and avoided pinning my hopes on even finishing this at all to prevent disappointment.

You'd think as someone who primarily makes my living by the pen I'd have figured this stuff out by now...

Even as I pen these lines I am still not certain if this piece will be ready in time. When you live with an executive functioning disorder, every day is like Russian roulette—except in reverse. If you don't fire blanks, you're on a roll that day! Nevertheless, every day, you roll the chamber and you shoot anyway.

I'm sure there's a life lesson embedded in this somewhere, something about how wherever there is life there is hope, or that believing in yourself is the answer to what you miss, or that chutzpah is the real core of success. I don't know. I've long ago stopped trying to sum up my worldview and philosophy in Hallmark card formats. Something is always lost in translation.

Perhaps it seems like a somewhat irresponsible way to live. Why not make a writing schedule or something? Set an alarm? Why not apply some discipline? I guess the best response to that is: I'm neurodivergent. This is how I work best. I've learned not to argue with my own brain.

But for many years I would have done exactly that.

Through the serious misapplication of some common wisdom regarding careful planning and steely discipline I was for many years exceedingly effective in driving myself to produce enormous success in my life. I understand why it is a popular piece of advice to give people like me who struggle to get things done or to start them...but I'd like to convey to my reader a warning about the dangers of such advice when given to the non-normative individual, because while some may find this advice character building, I found it destroyed my entire sense of self.

I refer of course to the practice of autistic masking and the transgender behavior of passing as cisgender, which, for expedience, I'm just going to bundle in right underneath the term masking. For me, the two are one movement, not two.

Masking is the practice of using the autistic gift for pattern recognition, mimicry, and other clever ways of problem solving to devise strategies for performing the role of a neurotypical/cis-heteronormative person while indeed not being that sort of person at all.

In short, I was a very accomplished fake normal person.

I finished school with university exemption, two As, a B and a C. I was a trained classical musician, a novice stage performer, and minor local celebrity. I got my diploma at college *cum laude* and finished at the top of my class. I ran for class representative at college and ended up ascending to the position of department student representative council chairperson. I won the best student award for my final year of study. I performed as a vocalist entertainer for the Miss College pageant and in the musical that was performed at the national theater during celebrations of the college's 25th birthday.

There was, apparently, nothing in the way of my bright future, and everyone assumed I was set to go into the performing arts or one of the sciences.

But in my second year at college I gained 45 kgs of weight in a year. I did not notice this at the time—indeed my preference for loose comfortable clothing and my utter lack of interest in dolling-up my appearance meant that the only clue that tipped me off to this sudden physical transformation was the two student cards for my first and second year, side by side. It was something of a shock, both because it had happened and because I somehow had not noticed it happening.

Nowadays, I understand that this sort of thing is rather common among both transgender and autistic people perhaps due to body dysmorphia or a lack of proprioception of body awareness or other such factors.

But at the time it just seemed I had inexplicably blown up like a balloon overnight.

To this day, I still don't know what it was that caused this sudden and unusually rapid weight gain. I have never lost that weight, and my health has never recovered from whatever it was that went wrong that year. I now live on a disability grant and have had to make peace with the reality that whatever capacity for work I might have once had is gone now and the vagaries of approaching middle age are upon me. Coming to an acceptance of my physical and mental limitations was a process of learning to listen to my body and to my soul and becoming comfortable with the fact that normality was never going to be something I could strive for.

I do know that whatever it is that failed in my body failed because of extreme stress. My blood pressure, at 18, was already high enough to warrant medication, and more and more health issues kept piling up over time, all attributable at least in part to the effects of stress on the body. With time, I have come to understand that the particular genetics of our community make us vulnerable to certain physical health problems and chronic illnesses that most people won't ever experience, at least not until advanced old age, and that managing our stress and workload is an important part of ensuring we don't fall prey to those issues early on.

Unfortunately, the message reached me too late to help me prevent the onset of lifelong chronic illness. That horse has bolted, and the best I can do now is try to adapt to the reality that my capacity for the average sort of work people do will never match that of an able-bodied person ever again. My survival hinges on understanding what my limitations are, respecting and accommodating them as best I can, and figuring out what kind of work a body like mine is capable of. Like someone reaching retirement age, I have to accept the stage of my life as it is.

How did it get this bad for someone who is only 35 years old?

Well, it might be because I have been running on adrenaline from the time I could recite nursery rhymes out loud in public. Before every choir performance, piano recital, poetry recital, and stage play I had dry heaves in the bathroom...but what few people realized was the reason I could make such a flawless showing on stage despite that anxiety was because I did that every time I stepped outside my bedroom door. In reality, there was a lighter more pervasive form of the same stage fright lingering with me in every aspect of my daily life from the moment I woke until the moment I went to bed.

I was, by all accounts, a genius. But underneath that genius ran an undercurrent of terrible fragility that only came closer and closer to the surface as I grew older. The older I became the harder it became for me to sustain the terrible weight of this constructed persona I had borne that brought me so many accolades.

The first cracks in the facade came the year before I graduated high school. I had stopped sleeping properly and would sit up until well after midnight each night desperately trying to keep up with my homework. It was always, *always* done on time, even if it meant working through every lunch break and waking moment of my day—which I sometimes did.

That success was built on some rather backbreaking work for a teenager. I spent every waking moment either working, studying, practicing, or preparing to work, study, practice, or doing chores and necessary self-care.

Four hours of piano practice, or participation in competitive extramurals. Three hours of homework. A half hour of jogging stairs. A half hour three times a day to eat. Seven hours of sleep. Two hours on grooming, bathing, and housekeeping. Seven hours of school. Fun. No fun. What is that stuff?

I never skipped a single day of school unless I was booked off by my doctor. I never flunked a test. I never got less than an A, until that one year. When it happened, I could not stop weeping and got sent to the school psychologist for a talk about workload and expectations. This was the first time my cognitive disabilities would not give sway to my willpower. I dropped from a higher grade math class to standard grade, and got some sleep.

You see, beyond merely seeming to be neurotypical, my genius was also my mask. Underneath it I could hide all the strange and wonderful ways of my brain, glossed over with my sharp intellect to normalize my responses, and flawlessly portrayed by my stage-perfected method acting.

Far from being some enormous boon, my intelligence was my prison.

When I finally began to collapse entirely under the weight of performing not only in a neurotypical and cisnormative way but also as a genius for those around me, I went down hard and fast. Within five years of graduation, I was institutionalized for the first time after a mental breakdown.

As I grew older over the years, and more and more desperate to recapture the glory of my childhood and youth, I pushed myself harder and harder to try to perform again that genius everyone expected of me.

More than anyone, I expected it of myself. I felt a total and utter failure, a disappointment to the family that sacrificed so much to give me every possible opportunity—music lessons, drama lessons, choir lessons, art lessons, weekly extra classes at the gifted child center. And here I was, at best working for subminimum wage once or twice a week and chugging back psychiatric medications like they were smarties.

It took 33 years of wandering in this wilderness to discover that I was autistic and transgender. In the interim I lived in utter desolation of self.

I spent 15 of those years in a failed and utterly toxic marriage. I lived for years with crushing isolation and loneliness with only the most fairweather friends to stand by me. For decades, I ran around desperately trying everything I could think of—therapy, a small pharmaceutical arsenal of medications, motivational courses, new and better diaries, task managers, and professional organizers, and changing career paths over and over and over—but to no avail.

It all ended up hinging on a twist of fate: I fell in love with a transgender woman and it ripped up the fabric of my world.

In the path of loving her I learned about being transgender in a way that few people ever get to without entering transition for themselves. I also was challenged to discover new depths within myself as a partner supporting someone through the most heart-wrenching emotional torture I ever saw anyone endure—severe gender dysphoria. My marriage, rocky to begin with, did not survive this new affair, despite our genuine commitment to the tenets of polyamory. Ultimately, the contrast between this all-consuming and wholesome passion between soulmates and the toxic, painfully stuttering relationship with my first partner that had labored under the weight of both our traumas was one I could not delude myself about for very long.

With the dissolving of that relationship came a complete reinvention of self. My physical health, pushed to breaking point by the years of unmitigated stress, hit a new low, and I spent two years in a wheelchair, fighting for a way back out of the pit of my chronic physical and mental illness.

My lover literally pushed me through, sometimes covering several kilometres on foot pushing that wheelchair to support me. In that visceral demonstration of affection, I found tangible security and companionship with another person for the first time in my life, and, during that time, therapy I'd been repeating over and over finally landed home and I woke up one day understanding in a profound core way that I was genuinely loved, lovable, and lovely.

It helped me see things in myself more clearly, and as I began to realize who I was on the inside, who I really could be when I wasn't hiding myself, I found that there had been autistic and queer people around me all the time right there to welcome me.

I do not think I'd have ever had the nerve to confront the profound, crippling pain of the past that lay behind my masking to face the full reality of my gender identity, my neurodivergencey, and the traumas of my childhood if I had not found that sense of personal emotional security through my partner.

Truly, we are transformed through relationship.

Finally, I could face the thing that had hidden on the periphery of my awareness my whole life—the great truth underneath the great lie.

I was never like the others around me. In some way that for all of my eloquence I could not put a name to, I was always the other. I was always, even before I understood the concept or had words for it, queer and autistic.

I wish I'd known.

I wish that as a child my parents had not tried so hard to eradicate the part of me that caused my developmental psychologist to recommend that I should be placed in a special school.

I wish that I had known about other queer people and met them and spoken about them with my parents and that it would have been safe to describe to them the inner reality of my queerness that had hovered in the corner of my awareness since I was a toddler.

I wish I'd been able to tell my doctors some of the strange things about how my mind works in the beautiful, perfect words I have found now that I am part of the autism community instead of being driven to use neurotypical terms to describe a non-neurotypical existence and then getting misdiagnosed and stuffed full of pills that further ruined my health.

I wish I had known there were other people like me, people who I could talk to and hang out with who weren't such hard work to be around and who understood what I had to say even when I had no words.

I wish I had known what it means to be non-binary, that there were options for people like me too, and that it was possible for me to have a body and a life that reflected who I was on the inside: neither a woman nor a man.

I wish I'd known that there was a place in the world for me so that I could have gone looking for it sooner instead of spending half of my natural life expectancy feeling utterly alone in the world.

I wish I'd known people who helped me figure out who I was instead of people who tried to tell me who I was supposed to be.

I wish, more than anything, that I'd known I was transgender and autistic sooner.

I wish I'd not lost so much time finding my way home.

---

*Chris's profile is the stock image used to illustrate the term "high strung." That just means they are a born tightrope walker and don't fear heights.*

# Late to the Party

Hayden James (he/him/his)

Being both transgender and autistic are two quite different things to wrestle at once. Both are but an aspect of many factors that make a person who they are. Sometimes they may clash, but for many people who are both trans and autistic, the two mesh together in quite interesting ways. There are many ways to be trans, as well as many, many ways of being autistic, and no two people are identical. Both are quite wide spectrums, after all.

Often, transgender people know or have known that they're trans from when they were very young. Often, autistic people get recognized and diagnosed during their childhood.

I, however, feel that I arrived rather late to the party when it comes to discovering both of these sides of myself—discovering that I was both trans and autistic.

During my childhood, I knew something was different. Maybe it was my baffling bluntness or weirdly specific interests. Maybe it was the fact that I learned to read and write by looking over my brother's shoulder at the age of four. Maybe it was my, in some people's eyes, ridiculous sensitivities that other kids didn't seem to have. Maybe it was the fact that I only learned how to be properly social around the sixth or seventh grade. Maybe even the fact that I found almost anything remotely feminine-coded repulsive and would start crying if anybody tried to put me in a dress.

Or, perhaps it was all of the above.

As a child, I had no words for these feelings or my sense of self. In my head I was, for the most part, just a child. I rarely ever gave it more thought than the fact that I felt uncomfortable in dresses and the color pink. I was a rambunctious kid who climbed trees, played games with my two brothers, and collected just about anything remotely interesting that I would find on my way, like a starry-eyed magpie. I was also a sensitive kid, retreating to my own inner world with pen and paper when the outside world was too loud or too close. My younger brother (who was diagnosed with autism in his childhood) and my own worlds would often overlap and we developed a common language of sorts, quietly playing with each other or alone, while our older brother would play with other children. In hindsight, I think we have so much in common and understand each other so well because we are both on the spectrum, but that's an entirely different story.

Once puberty knocked on the door, the real dread arrived. There were so many unwanted and at times scary changes that would flood over a kid completely unprepared for them. Things were suddenly out of place, and lumps and bumps would appear in places where no lumps and bumps were supposed to be. On top of that, these changes appeared way ahead of my fellow classmates. It was dreadful whenever clothes were too tight and would reveal everything, so my form was almost always hidden away under hoodies or oversized shirts. These were also the times where some things became clearer than they ever were: I felt out of place among the girls and unwelcome among the boys (despite relating to them more) but I still did not know what these feelings meant.

Around my 17th rotation around the Earth, during just another day of roaming the internet, I ran into the terms transgender, non-binary, and dysphoria. Reading more about what these words meant, something clicked, as I finally found words for what had pestered me this whole time. I related so much to the boys because I perceived myself as being one of them.

Many transgender people whom I befriended or read about seemed to have known when they were much younger. It felt weird to meet people who had known for so long, while I had only just found out, but it felt good to be a step closer in the process of understanding myself.

So when I could afford it and got up the courage, I came out to my closest friends and bought my first binder.

Putting on a binder for the first time, when you already have poor coordination, was like dancing an awkward tango with yourself, while getting a hug that was too tight. Despite this, it hid away the thing that was causing me the most distress, and a temporary relief would wash over me. It wasn't ideal, however, to have to wrestle into a sleeveless straightjacket every time dysphoria knocked on the door and I had to face the outside world. I felt restricted by the lumps on my chest, like they were keeping me from looking like and doing the things that I wanted to do.

But it was a big change and by the power of overthinking, many talks with my therapist, and the support from my mother and friends, as well as overcoming my fear of strangers cutting into my body, I slowly but surely started my transition.

During this whole debacle, however, something was still left unaddressed. At several points of my life, I was suffering from bouts of depression and anxiety, both because of the dysphoria, as well as a world being too demanding, loud, bright, and close for my comfort. I would cry a lot and for the most part it was just written off as being "too sensitive" or "too childish," which only fuelled the bullies' urge to target me. In that sense, I was sensitive, but nothing was really done about it, because I was able to keep up with school just fine, get good grades, and be social with the few friends I did have. Along with an increasing pressure to figure out what career to pursue, as well as my family being slowly torn in two by a messy divorce while I was entering high school, however, all these factors were too much and almost ended my life.

Had it not been for the small handful of really close friends I had amassed during my teen years who supported me, I wouldn't have been able to make it through high school, let alone be here right now.

After a particularly dark time that prompted two of my friends to drag me to the closest psychiatric emergency ward, I finally got therapy. It was something that I had desperately needed, but never thought that I was worthy of.

I had often been very curious of the autism spectrum and would often research it in order to be able to understand and help my little brother. But the more I read about it, the more I found myself relating to the experiences that other autistic people had. Reading the, mostly, common symptoms of the condition also proved to be awfully close to the way I experienced the world. Looking back on my childhood, there were many things on the list that stuck out: the intense fixation on interests, the difficulty I would often have filtering out sensory input, resulting in distress (or, as I now found out to be, meltdowns); the tendency to often lack understanding of social cues and expressions, as well as shying away from social situations; the need for careful planning and crystal clear instructions; the verbal tics and stimming... the list went on.

Since I was assigned female at birth and socialized as such (or however you would put this), I also explored the often overlooked symptoms of girls on the spectrum as well, since the focus has often been on symptoms seen in boys. One of those on that list stuck out particularly: mirroring.

Now I will neither say that I am completely inept in social situations, nor will I claim that I'm an expert. When I met my closest and now oldest friend in sixth grade (whom I will refer to as A) I knew only so much about interactions. Thus far, I had only been close friends with one other person, whom I drifted apart from many years ago. But in this friend, in A, I had someone whom I could refer to during social interactions. A was at that point a shy kid like me, but had a much easier grasp of talking to others, and as such I saw what they did and tried out the same. A introduced me to new people and I would awkwardly implement what I saw and heard, and joke away when I was at loss for what else to do, like a chameleon comedian. It worked—surprisingly—and slowly but surely a closely knit social group formed around me. Before I knew it, I became the one to also introduce people to each other and at times even initiate the banter, but I still desperately craved time alone.

I have no doubt in my heart that A is the reason that I'm able to be as social as I am today. A was also one of the first that I came out to as trans. In many ways, they changed my life for the better.

Back then, I did not know that I was autistic. I would often consider if I was, but I never felt that I could apply that diagnosis to myself. Everyone has their quirks after all.

What truly seemed to hammer the nail into place was one particular talk on the kitchen floor with my mother. It was a warm summer afternoon around two years ago, where she mentioned to me that I in fact was autistic. Apparently, both of my brothers and I had been screened at a young age. Both my little brother and I were on the spectrum, but since I was more "high functioning," no further actions were taken.

I decided to share this newfound discovery with my new therapist and thus, after many therapy sessions, correspondences between them and my mum, and a psychologist specialized in diagnosing, I was officially diagnosed (more specifically with Asperger's syndrome) at the ripe age of 22. The last puzzle piece finally seemed to click, like an answer to a question you already know, but had at the tip of your tongue the whole time. The people around me felt the same way, because the more they learned about autism, the more sense the little quirks in my behavior started making. I count my lucky stars every day for having friends who are as kind, welcoming, and understanding as they are.

But what does being trans mean to me? And how does it mesh with also being autistic, in my case at least?

At its core, being transgender generally means to transition from one gender, the one you were assigned at birth, to another. Usually this is seen as transitioning from male to female and vice versa, but I don't believe there's one set way to be trans. When discovering the term non-binary for the first time, I felt that there was something that described my experience perfectly. As I never felt truly at home with either male or female, at first I thought that non-binary was the end-all answer to my woes.

It's something I've found to have in common with a surprising number of autistic transgender people, as the rigid binary doesn't always perfectly describe our experience. Quite a few of us see ourselves as...well, ourselves, which doesn't always mean male or female. Even after coming to terms with my identity as a trans man in the end, it never really was a dramatic revelation or a huge declaration. I was just me: a very peculiar, ambiguous man, but a man nonetheless. I told the ones that I felt this information was relevant to and left it at that. If people weren't going to budge on the way they viewed me, it would be their problem. It took a lot of self-reflection, but I'm glad I gave it the extra thought. Well, I was going to overthink it regardless, but you get the idea.

There are many things I'm still very uncertain about: where my place in the world is, what the future might bring, whether I should get the sugary cereal with the bright packaging that my brain and taste buds are begging me to get, or stick with the oatmeal with fruits and nuts that I usually eat in the mornings. But these two aspects of me, being transgender and autistic, are two certain constants that always were there and always will be, even if I was a little late to join the party. Just two more pieces of a whole me.

---

*Hayden is a fun-loving Danish–Caribbean lad. He loves the ocean, writing stories, making art and comics, and playing Pokémon. He also enjoys making new friends.*

# The Rightness of Being Wrong

*Baden Gaeke Franz (they/them/theirs)*

The first thing you learn in a women's and gender studies class is that gender is a social construct. The very existence of gender is not objectively observable by any scientific measure we know. If you ask a gender studies professor what gender is, they will tell you that gender is not necessarily tied to any physical or mental characteristics, sexual identity, social role, choice of clothing or job, or any of the many other characteristics we usually associate with gender. Gender is none of those things, they tell you. What they do not tell you is what gender is if it is not that.

2000: I am five years old. There is a trans boy in my kindergarten class. I don't have a concept of that yet. I know he wants to be a boy but in my mind he is still a girl. I ask him questions about his genitals so I can know if he is a boy or a girl. I don't know anything about gender yet, but I know that boys have penises and girls do not.

My mother says she knew I was autistic from the moment she saw me. She never had me diagnosed because she didn't want to "other" me and she didn't think it would affect her decisions about how to parent me. So I grew up knowing I was different from the other kids around me, but not having any idea why. I think maybe it's because they all watch TV and I do not. I spend elementary school feeling lost and alone and never having any friends.

2002: I am seven years old. My favorite color is pink because it is a girl color. My second favorite colors are red and purple because they are close to pink. I prefer to be around women than men because I am a girl like them. I am the epitome of a good young girl.

There is a common narrative in trans communities about always knowing you were different. Being born in the wrong body. Always wanting to play with the wrong toys or wanting friends who were the wrong gender. Those narratives never quite fit me. As a child, I was perfectly happy to be a girl. That was the way things were, and so that's what I did. I wasn't born in the wrong body. I became wrong for the body I was born in.

2005: I am ten years old. My special interest is Canadian athlete and cancer activist Terry Fox. I do not know what a special interest is yet, but I know I love him. I dress up as him for Halloween. I know he's a boy but I still want to be him. My mother says, "He was an amazing man." That feels different. Being a boy feels okay. Being a man somehow feels weird. I dress up as him anyway.

Since I didn't know I was trans from the moment I was born, I sometimes feel like I'm not trans enough. Like I'm faking it because I haven't known I was trans as long as many of my trans friends have. I got a late start to understanding I was trans, so therefore my identity is fake. Wrong. I am not allowed to explore gender because to do so is to appropriate transness from the people who did it right.

2010: I am 15 years old. My close friend from school comes out as a trans man. Around the same time, a different friend comes out as non-binary. I am oblivious enough not to notice for months. But when I do, I become a firm defender of both of them. My views of gender as static disappear. The trans man changes his name so often that my family jokingly refers to him as "he who cannot be named."

In high school, I found my people. We were a group of misfits who all found each other and loved and supported one another. Looking back, everybody in that group was queer, neurodivergent, or both. Mostly both. Through this group, I stopped feeling different and started feeling like one of a group. We are not like most people, but we are also not alone. Not wrong.

2011: I am 16 years old. My church youth group leader asks us to stand on a spectrum from how much we feel like a man or like a woman. I stand in the middle. For some reason, I forget this incident until years later when I'm thinking about how I never had a feeling of being trans as a child.

In 1990, Judith Butler[49] wrote that gender is a performance. It is not an objective observable thing, but rather an act people put on to allow others to read them as male or female, masculine or feminine. Gender can therefore only be understood within the context of individual performance. Every person who performs femininity defines it for themselves, and the choices they make in that performance inform the way other women choose to perform their own femininity. We define gender as we act it out.

2012: I am 17 years old. I go on a trip to Europe with my class. One of my other autistic friends has a meltdown due to the stress of the trip, which manifests in yelling about how gender can't change and she can't be around my trans friend any more. She is stressed that something she thought was static could change. My friendship group breaks up over it. I am the only one who still talks to everybody on both sides. I almost burn out myself. (Years in the future, she will discover that she herself is non-binary and part of her stress came from his transness forcing her to examine her own gender and discovering the wrongness there.)

The problem with the definition of gender as performance is that it does not help me to understand my own relationship with gender. Gender is performance. Okay. But what exactly is the nature of that performance? What precisely does somebody have to do or say to be a woman? To be a man? My autistic brain understands things by breaking them down into pieces, examining the pieces, then reassembling them into the whole to understand the whole. But gender cannot be understood this way. The pieces are just as nebulous and undefinable as the whole is.

2013: I am 18 years old. I take an introduction to gender studies class taught by a trans woman. She explains that gender is different from gender role. I feel relief because I can be a girl but still fit masculine gender roles. I didn't want to be trans, but I know I don't fit into the box of "woman." If I can be a masculine woman maybe that will be enough. Maybe I don't have to be wrong after all. If you have to make deals with yourself about your gender, it's usually a signal that your gender isn't what you think it is.

I discovered I was autistic in my first year of university. My special interest at the time was the podcast *Welcome to Night Vale*, and I strongly related to the character of Carlos. When I looked at fan blogs about the show, people talked about how they also related to Carlos because he had autistic traits and so did they. I started to do research into autism from the perspective of autistic people. Suddenly a lifetime of feeling different made sense. I wasn't wrong. I was autistic.

2014: I am 19 years old. A server at a restaurant calls me sir. My friends try to reassure me that it's okay and I'm a beautiful woman. But inside I'm happy to know I could pass for male if I wanted to. I still think about that waiter from time to time, even years later. There is no cisgender explanation for that.

I got my formal autism diagnosis a few days before my 20th birthday. I didn't really need the services or accommodations that came with it at that point. I had been living without them for so long. For me, a diagnosis was a pass to join the autistic community, make friends, and do advocacy work. I threw myself into the autistic community, happy at last to have found people like myself.

2015: I am 20 years old. I send a message to my non-binary friend, asking them about their gender and how they knew they were non-binary. I tell them that I'm generally neutral about my body but occasionally love it and occasionally hate it. I am scared to tell anybody I'm non-binary because I am afraid they will judge me. I remember the nickname "he who cannot be named" and cringe. It's not so funny when it's me.

The more time I spent with autistic people, the more I realized exactly how many of us were trans and non-binary. I started to wonder if my own feelings of confusion around defining my own gender were more universal than I had thought. The more I thought about it the more it made sense. Gender isn't objective or observable. Of course people like me who have difficulty with abstract concepts would find it confusing!

2016: I am 21 years old. I am dating somebody who identifies as lesbian. One night she tells me that she would still love me if I was a boy. I hug her tighter and almost cry. I don't fully understand why it means so much to hear that, but I know that it doesn't make sense for me to feel this way if I were truly a woman.

I brought up the observation that autistic people seemed more likely to be trans to some neurotypical mothers of autistic kids, and was immediately shut down. They claimed my observations were the result of confirmation bias and that I only thought there were more trans autistic people because I spent so much time around trans people. I knew that couldn't be the only factor, but I couldn't convince them. They were invested in autistic people not being trans. I still don't entirely understand why.

2017: I am 22 years old. I start to have bad dysphoria days more often. I start buttoning my flannels and tucking them into my pants. It hides my chest better. I join some online trans forums and start going by "they" in explicitly queer spaces, but I remain terrified to come out in any places I am less sure about. I've heard the stories and I know what they do to people like me.

When I started looking into grad school, I remembered the intersections of trans and autistic identity that I had noticed, and the reluctance of neurotypical mothers to believe me when I talked about it. I decided that this would be a good thesis topic and started researching it. What I found confirmed my suspicions: article after article explaining that autistic people are anywhere from three to ten times as likely to be trans compared with the average population. I felt validated. I wasn't alone and I wasn't making this up. Trans autistic people did exist, and we existed in significantly large enough numbers for researchers to ask why. Despite what the neurotypical mothers said, my lived experiences matched the literature. They were the ones who were wrong.

2018: I am 23 years old. I decide that if gender is a performance, I should learn to perform masculinity better to match my new masculine identity. I consult men's style blogs and advice columns, but they give advice that is unhelpful at best and openly misogynistic at worst. I turn to the Netflix show *Queer Eye*, knowing they give advice to men and trusting gay men more than straight men to give advice that isn't toxic. What I find instead is an incredibly diverse group of people who are all men. I learn that just as I don't have to reject my masculine traits to be a woman, I also don't have to reject my feminine traits to not be a woman.

A common trait in autistic people, particularly those assigned female at birth, is hyper-empathy. We have difficulty telling the difference between our own emotions and those of others, but rather than assuming that others feel the way we do, we assume we feel as they do. We take their emotions and their very beings into our own selves. When I gained a special interest in Disney's *Newsies*, I entered fan spaces surrounding them. Fan spaces discussing the possibility of trans characters. Young people exploring their own transness. I found myself feeling more masculine than I had before. Because I was taking on their stories? Because they were validating my own? How do I tell the difference? Does the difference even matter?

2019: I am 24 years old. I come out as non-binary in most areas of my life. I am scared to do it. I have heard stories about terrible things happening to trans people when they come out. But nothing happens. I keep my job. My family still loves me. My professors respect my pronouns. I still feel scared and vulnerable sometimes when I talk about my gender, but it's slowly getting easier.

As I write this I remain uncertain. Gender remains a mystery to me—both my own gender and the concept of gender as a whole. My gender is not a fixed thing. It is alive just as much as I am. A history I rewrite every day. But I know I'm not alone. We are in this together. All of us. Navigating the mystery side by side, helping each other through the hard times. Knowing that even in our wrongness, we are right.

---

*Baden is a non-binary academic and lifelong student from Canada. They are an autistic self-advocate and founding board member of Autistics United Canada.*

# Finding Validity at Work

*Kevvie Vida (she/her/hers)*

Hi, it's me, Kevvie! This is one of my many catchphrases. I use it anytime I walk into a room and online at the start of most messages. Often in conversation I rely on a set of catchphrases; it's far easier to have a handful of words and phrases to respond with than to come up with responses on the spot. Another one I use frequently is "yay," which I'll say in a variety of intonations depending on context, and often comes across as ironic or sarcastic. Sarcasm is difficult for me to understand, though. Most conversations I interpret literally, unless the sarcasm is terribly obvious. This can lead to a lot of confusion on my part. It is also confusing when I say something and it is interpreted as sarcasm because, I don't know why—maybe I used the wrong tone? Conversations are tough, that's why I stick with my go-to responses. Yay!!! Hugs!

I didn't realize I was transgender until I was 19. Looking back, there were obvious indications, but at the time I didn't have the understanding or the language to express it. When I was in middle school, when I first thought I was gay, on top of being terrified, I felt a wave of relief; I may not be a girl, but since I'm gay I'm as close as I can be to being a girl. My friends called me an honorary girl. In high school, I made a viral YouTube video in drag, but it got too popular for my school to handle and I received death threats. They forced me to take down the video, put the dress in the back of the closet, and I was told I could never dress like that again, for the sake of my safety. Sadly, I was stuck being a gay boy till I got to college.

Brace yourself—the next part of this story is unusual and kind of lame, but it's my story. We were discussing Virginia Woolf in class, and as an exercise our professor made us change seats for the day, men on one side of the room, women on the other side. He then proceeded to hand out chocolates and napkins to the men, and saltines and single-ply tissue paper to the women. The guys immediately started talking shit like they were entitled to have the chocolates, and the women were arguing about how bullshit the guys were behaving. I had a terrible internal struggle in this moment. Sitting with the guys, looking across the room, I felt as if I belonged on the other side of the table. What the men were saying disgusted me, and I agreed with the women. But it was more than just an agreement, it was my moment of realization. As soon as class ended I texted my friend, "I think I'm a woman."

It was several more years before I understood I was autistic. As long as I can remember I've wondered if I were autistic. However, growing up, my step-brother had a developmental disability, and my parents enforced the idea that because I was not like my step-brother, I was neurotypical; since my disability didn't manifest itself the way it did in my step-brother it was and continues to be dismissed. For years, I questioned my place on the spectrum, but still felt as if it couldn't be legitimate. A few autistic friends were affirming of my suspicions; I have a hard time trusting my own feelings and intuition, so getting that outside validation really helped cement it for me. Perhaps I really was autistic. The more I read, the more lightbulbs went on, another set of dots connected, and I was finally making sense to myself. Finally, when a friend sent me the call for submissions for this book, and it said "most autistics know who they are once they've learned what autism is," and that self-identification is valid, then I finally felt confident in claiming it.

I have a hard ass time talking about emotions; I don't understand why it is so hard for me but it is. Often I have a delayed emotional response to events. My brain takes a while to process the stimulus in a way that makes sense to me. Sometimes it can take days or even weeks before I realize something hurt me. After I realize I'm upset I also have a difficult time articulating what I'm feeling. Because of this, I'm very bad at talking to people about their emotions. As much as I want to be there for people to talk to, I seem to fall short. I would much rather be a physical presence for someone, a hand to hold, a shoulder to cry on, a hug. That stuff is much easier than using words. However, most of my interpersonal interactions are online, so I can't be a physical presence. Usually I'll say something like "I'm sorry you're having such a hard time right now" followed by "Hugs!" If I can't hug them in person I could at least send them a virtual hug. Unfortunately, "Hugs" is not the most helpful response, and I've lost a few friends because I wasn't able to communicate in a deeper way than that when they were struggling.

I work at a local Lush store. Lush Fresh Handmade Cosmetics is a progressive company that puts its ethics at the forefront of everything it does; fighting animal testing, minimal packaging, ethical sourcing, and so on. Lush is the perfect place for me to work because all my intersecting identities are able to flourish. In 2018, Lush launched the "Trans Rights Are Human Rights" campaign. During this campaign, Lush raised almost half a million dollars for trans-led organizations in North America. It also distributed 75 thousand booklets on how to be a trans ally. Not only is Lush trans-friendly on the corporate level, but these core values run through each individual store. When I was asked invasive questions in the break room at work, the managers shut that shit down immediately and pulled me aside to say they supported me and would stand by me one hundred percent. My transness will always be valid and respected at Lush.

Lush is also one of the few companies I'm aware of that celebrates drag queens. In the 2018 holiday campaign "DRAGmas," three Chicago-based drag queens, Kim Chi, Shea Couleé, and Detox, were hired to promote the seasonal products. These queens were featured in videos, on social media, and even had giant cutout displays at the front of every store! Several Lush locations across the country also hosted meet and greets for these queens! When I wanted to go to work in drag, they said that since Lush policy allows employees to wear their makeup however they please, it was fair game. As long as my outfit complied with the Lush dress code—everything besides accessories must be black or white—I could show up to work as extravagant as I pleased! Of course, when it was time to work in drag, I chose more practical options, like flats instead of eight-inch heels. Working at Lush in drag was a blast and helped attract people to our store from off the street. I'm lucky to work somewhere that encourages my passion for drag.

I've had several years to learn who I am as a trans person, but I'm just starting the journey of learning who I am as an autistic person. Discovering these two facets of my identity has helped me better understand myself, and I've found a supportive community that embraces all aspects of me. I hope moving forward in my journey I'll continue to find support as I become even more confident in living authentically.

---

*Kevvie is a 25-year-old drag queen from Chicago. She is currently completing her master's degree and plans to one day open a drag museum.*

# Reflections

HDG (she/her/hers or they/them/theirs)

How do I know I'm autistic? I didn't know for 43 years, so how do I know it now? It's more than trusting a diagnosis; after all, I sought that out myself, as confirmation of my own suspicions. Those suspicions took time to grow, as I encountered more and more descriptions—of lives, of senses, of bodies and minds in motion—that hinted at where I belonged. I knew all along that I was different, but I didn't have words to define that difference, words that allowed me to seek out others whose differences resonated with mine.

How do I know I'm trans? In similar ways, I have only recently found the words to define a difference I have felt my entire life: not girl, not boy, not woman, not man. I have sometimes tried to explain that I felt like "both," or "neither," and I have always found it jarring to be referred to as a woman. Encountering other people's stories of being similarly outside the gender binary has given me new frames of reference, and shown me options I hadn't seen before.

These reflections of myself in other people's experiences have helped solidify my own sense of identity as an autistic person, and as a non-binary trans person. Sociology describes identity formation as a social process; we learn who we are through the lens of other people. But for both trans and neurodivergent people, what is reflected back by the dominant culture often does not resonate with our own experiences. Finding other people's stories in which we can see ourselves can be a powerful help in discovering who we really are.

It took me decades to find stories like that, however, and, in the meantime, I absorbed a lot of messages that blocked this kind of self-exploration, especially when it came to gender. I remember telling my mother once that I didn't feel like a girl. She asked if I felt like a boy, and I said no, not really. I could tell by the relief in her response that this was the "right" answer, and that other answers were not okay to explore. I don't remember how old I was, but I was young, maybe nine or ten years old. I didn't bring it up again, but that feeling never went away.

Later, in my early teens, I wanted to get my hair cut short. To be honest, I wanted to look like Michelle Pfeiffer in *Ladyhawke*, a 1985 fantasy movie about a woman who is a hawk by day, traveling medieval France with her lover, and a man who is a wolf by night. I loved that movie and her character, who wore her hair in short, tousled layers; I thought it made her look so free and fearless, and I liked how effortless it looked compared to my own long hair. But I was embarrassed about the inspiration for my haircut, so I just tried to describe what I wanted to the hairdresser—how long it was, how it angled across the sides, and so on. When she asked me questions, I tried to remember more details, but mostly kept coming back to the same few points. I was starting to realize that I just wanted it short, maybe even shorter than Michelle's, but that met some resistance.

At one point the hairdresser, frowning, asked me, "Like a boy cut?" and I recoiled. Her tone was so clearly negative and disapproving that I quickly said, "No, just...short." Then I just wanted to get out of there as quickly as possible, so I said yes to all the rest of her suggestions. The resulting haircut was a disaster, of course; all of the natural waves in my hair, which had been barely noticeable when it was long and heavy, took over and made odd shapes on my head that were hard to tame. It ended up taking more work to keep in line than my long hair had ever required, which left me very frustrated. I learned later that my hair needs to be a lot shorter for me to be happy with it, but at the time that was unthinkable. That was a "boy cut," something that I wanted but was clearly wrong for me to have.

So I toed the line, at least for a while. Sociologists often refer to gender as a performance, and I have certainly performed "woman" even if I didn't feel like one. This blends with the autistic experience of "masking" or "camouflaging," in which we try to pass as non-autistic by mimicking the dominant neurotype and suppressing our autistic traits. When I put on a mask to fit in, that fitting in is at least partly dictated by social expectations rooted in gender. And if the gender society puts on me is "woman," then "woman" becomes part of my mask. But is the mask convincing? Do I want it to be?

For a long time, I didn't realize I had anything to mask; I just knew I needed to play along with social rules if I wanted people to like and accept me. I studied those rules, not realizing how much harder I needed to work at that than other people did. There were always some rules I didn't accept, and a lot of those were gendered. I didn't feel as if they had to apply to me, but I could still feel the pressure to follow them in the way people reacted to me. In their eyes, my mask was incomplete.

Learning that I am autistic, and exploring what that means, has intertwined with learning what it means to be trans. I discovered that autistic people are more likely to be trans or otherwise gender noncon-forming than the typical population, and that got me thinking more deeply about my own gender. I started reading more and more about experiences similar to mine, and uncovered a profusion of words for genders outside the binary of man and woman. I embraced words like genderqueer, non-binary, and enby, and appreciated the ways in which others, like agender and genderfluid, helped me realize which ones did not fit me.

Reading specifically autistic experiences of being trans has been eye-opening. There are many types of trans narratives, many different trans journeys. The public, when aware of trans people at all, seems to see the story as a binary switch, a movement from man to woman,

woman to man. For some people this may indeed be the case, while for others things are much more blended, vague, fluid, or simply different from binary expectations. I have particularly encountered this in autistic narratives about gender, which have given me an expanded context in which to see myself and my sometimes-messy experience of gender.

I have encountered speculation that autistic people are less influenced by the social pressures that are brought to bear on gender variance; we either care less about society's "rules," or we simply miss the social signaling that aims to enforce them. I never cared for makeup, for example—it made my face itch, and I didn't like how it looked anyway. It just didn't make sense to me to wear it just because others did, so I didn't really care if they expected me to. I felt similarly about wearing dresses or other stereotypically "feminine" clothing; it wasn't comfortable and didn't feel right. Sometimes I was aware of gender expectations around how I dressed, such as when my mother insisted I wear a dress to some social event, but a lot of times I think it went right over my head.

I remember one incident from junior high school, when I was stopped by a girl and her friends. "Nice ensemble," she sneered, looking me up and down. I remember being aware that she was trying to be mean, but I was honestly confused by what she meant. I had only heard the word "ensemble" in a musical context, to describe one of the subgroups that performed in the school band. I wasn't in it, and at the moment I was walking alone, so...not part of an ensemble.

"What do you mean?" I asked.

She waved a hand at me. "All this," she said. I looked down at myself. I don't remember now what I saw, but I'm sure I was wearing jeans and some kind of comfortable top, maybe a t-shirt layered under something else. She and her friends were dressed more fashionably, their clothes and makeup more carefully considered and clearly feminine. I looked back up at her.

"My clothes?" I asked. She was starting to get impatient.

"Yes," she snapped. "They don't go together at all."

I blinked. I think I was still integrating the fact that "ensemble" had referred to what I was wearing, which overrode my annoyance that she had interrupted my walk to criticize my clothes. Obviously, this incident rankled enough to have stuck in my memory all this time, but only because I thought it was absurd. Only in hindsight does it strike me as an example of social pressure from others of my (presumed) gender; at the time I didn't get the message.

"Oh. Okay," I finally said, and continued on my way.

So sometimes social signals landed, and sometimes they didn't. I certainly didn't escape the socialization process, the constant reinforcement of a strictly binary gender arrangement (and the related reinforcement of which side of it I was on). Throughout my involvement in predominantly male environments—martial arts dojos, physics classes, the US military—I was constantly reminded that I wasn't just another student, peer, or colleague. I was "the girl." And when I found myself around women, we were an "all-female team," or "all ladies here." Either way, it never felt quite right.

When I learned that I'm autistic, it helped make sense of these experiences of not fitting in, especially as I encountered autistics expressing similar dissatisfaction with the gender binary. But then, too, I started reading more articles describing the "female" forms of autism. Many of these I related to, as I was socialized as female, and I think it's helpful to expand beyond one-size-fits-all descriptions of autism that are based solely on young boys. But then, those descriptions don't fit all males, either, and if autistic people are truly more likely to be gender variant than the general population, does creating lists of "male" and "female" autistic traits really make much sense?

Sometimes I find it alienating to encounter descriptions of "female" autism, even when I can see myself in them. At the same time, I can recognize many ways in which I still identify as female. (I still predominantly use she/her pronouns, for example.) I was socialized as female, seen and treated as a woman by others, and I still feel more comfortable in groups of women than groups of men. But not all the time; it really depends on how much those men or women project their gender expectations onto me. As I wrote on my blog once, "Thinking I'm a cis woman, men treat me as different even when I feel the same, and women treat me as the same even when I feel different." I suppose I feel most comfortable with those who don't treat gender as the primary organizing principle when deciding how to treat people.

I still perform the role of "woman" most of the time, or at least I don't always feel moved to correct that impression. But since learning I'm autistic, I've been working on unmasking, letting myself move and think and communicate in ways that feel more natural to me. That includes taking off parts of my gender mask that never felt like they belonged, parts I only added because they made other people more comfortable. Forging an authentic identity that embraces being both autistic and non-binary has been an ongoing process, and those two pieces feel deeply entangled. It is in autistic narratives that I find stories that match my own experience of gender, and in trans autistics that I see echoes of my autistic self, outside depictions of "male" or "female" autism. I see each one reflected in the other, and in those reflections I see myself.

---

*HDG is a 46-year-old, genderqueer autistic with endless curiosity. She lives in western Massachusetts and blogs at eclecticautistic.wordpress.com.*

# Definitions

*James J Myers (he/him/his or they/them/theirs)*

She:
to refer to a woman, girl, female.
A word I never thought would cause me so much discomfort, that it
    feels like my chest is exploding.
Like I'm not in my own body.
I feel that I'm just an empty form.

He:
Used to refer to a man, boy, male.
A word I never thought I'd identify as. Something I'd never think
    would cause me so much joy that it feels like I'm walking on air.
Like I'm one of the guys.
I feel that I finally belong.

Retard:
A word I was once called by other students when word got out of
    my "disability."
A word I never want to hear, yet constantly recognize it as it echoes
    through the school halls.
Like I'm some sort of charity case.
Yet I feel there is hope, even when my music doesn't drown the
    comments out.

I want to stay silent for I am afraid I will be shamed by students,
teachers, family members...strangers.
It is not an easy thing to be fully open. Especially with Asperger's.
Yet I cannot continue down this path.
My heart has become a shattered reflection of the person I once was.
My galaxy is now a pile of broken planets and stars.
I am here, patiently waiting for someone to sew me back together
with rainbow lace, call me J, and act as if I am normal.

Not a distressed doll with patches people gave me, not to fit my
needs, but theirs.
I know, some of you know this. You care, you know I exist, and
you're here for me.
But some of you are still left in the dark, and I am sorry for that.
But when 73 percent of transgender students have been subjects
of mockery, or 87 percent don't feel safe at school, it's hard to
be honest.
I cannot make you understand. I cannot force anything upon you.
That's not my goal.

My goal is to be honest with myself by being honest with you, and
to remind myself that being autistic and trans is not a curse,
but a gift.

So here I am, J, 17. A brother, a friend, a person.

He, him, his.

Not just autistic. Not just trans. Human as well.

---

*James is a teenager with Asperger's syndrome, from Ontario, Canada. He likes
art, music, and writing poetry, as well as standing up for LGBTQ+ rights.*

# A Transtistic Evolution

*Jordan (they/them/theirs or he/him/his)*

I mostly identify as queer. This is my current all-encompassing identity label. It includes my gender, sexuality, and my autistic traits quite well.

I have always been different, even when I was very young.

One of my very few childhood memories is of me, around the age of nine, climbing from the front to the back seat of my dad's car, landing on my groin, and exclaiming, "Oh my fucking balls!" I was laughed at and condescended to by my siblings.

I came out as bisexual in my mid-teens and came out as lesbian and stone butch in my early 20s directly after leaving an abusive husband—a husband I married because that was what society expected. I came out as transgender (female to male) in my mid-20s. In my late 20s, I started taking the hormone dehydroepiandrosterone (DHEA) without consulting a doctor and lived full time as male for two years, my "real-life test," as doctors call it.

I shared a house with a gay couple who knew me pre-transition during my "real-life test." After one of them sadly passed away, the remaining partner and I became intimate. My new partner was a "gay man who became bi for me," a phrase that I've heard spoken by many people—and that I despise. I feel that my new partner didn't really become bi for me, because he viewed me as male everywhere but behind closed doors and often then as well.

Through this relationship, I learned that I do not actually identify as a gay man.

At the time, I chose not to transition surgically or get testosterone, even though I qualified and was seeking out a gender specialist.

I made this personal choice for a few reasons. I was considering having more children and wanted to breastfeed from my own bosom. A phalloplasty cost $100,000 USD at the time, and required implants in order to work properly. Clitoral release was less expensive, but still cost money. Testosterone maintenance over a lifetime is also expensive, and insurance wouldn't cover it.

Through some of my spiritual practices, I learned about two-spirit people, and this suited me really well. I choose to walk in both worlds and neither, and now I mostly call myself genderfluid, gender neutral, andro(gynous), or genderqueer, with the latter being my preferred term. Even though I advocated that trans folks do not have to surgically transition to be valid, my own isms and self-doubt made me wonder if not transitioning while breeding would make me a fraud.

Sexually, I am pretty asexual I think—I believe it is called demi or grey. I'm not sure where exactly I fit on the ace spectrum because when I am in a new relationship there is a lot of "go at it like bunny rabbits" that eventually wanes and I can then go months or years without and be fine.

Also, different gender presentations have different attractions to me from power dynamic and physical attraction perspectives.

I can be sexually or physically attracted to various people—primarily male presenting, women, or trans and with distinct, amazingly distinct, types of attraction, including race and features. I suspect these distinct types are intertwined with my gender because while I truly date based on someone's heart, the initial physical attraction to someone walking down the street is interesting. There are some skin tones that generally only attract me in one gender presentation—or rather only elicit a physically noticeable immediate response of attraction.

Tied in to that...if I am having a "guy day" and am attracted to a female-presenting person, that feels heterosexual. But if it's not a guy day, it feels lesbian or queer. If a feminine-ish day and with a male-presenting person, it's the same feeling of heterosexuality. Once any internal gender dominates on a given day, it may fall into a different externally perceived sexuality category "by definition."

So yeah...I'm queer...and blessedly so. For now.

Now for the long version and then how this intertwines with my autistic identity. The two-year "real-life test" in my 20s had zero therapeutic support after many years of knowing I was trans but not being sure if I "qualified medically" to transition.

I had many long talks with a transitioning pre-op female-to-male (FTM) over those years. They were not transitioning at the time but are now.

I had two main issues with surgery. First, as mentioned before, bottom surgery was $100,000 USD for a dick that wouldn't work right without help. As someone who already had a low libido, the idea of excusing myself to pump, insert rods, and so on was mortifying and would have ruined sexual desire before I was physically ready. That, and the cost of maintenance was so high for FTMs. Even a metoidioplasty (clitoral release) would only allow me a micro penis, causing social and emotional anxiety. Top surgery has *always* been on the table.

Second, I have an adult child and though we do not speak anymore, I wanted more children and to breastfeed them as I had my eldest because I felt it was the right thing to do for them.

My current spouse is quite aware and open to whether I choose to transition fully or partially in the future. I may actually have a hysterectomy soon and if so we have discussed that I would like to have my ovaries removed as well so I can feel a little more "me." I am very fortunate having him in my life because my first husband (and father to my eldest) was an abusive, domineering, rapist, son-of-a-bitch. My current spouse is polyamorous, so if I do transition, we wouldn't dissolve the marriage.

My trans journey has given me a unique perspective because I have actually experienced white male privilege and transphobia depending on the circle of people I was around.

My "passing" was never an issue before and I often "pass" to this day, in my 40s, without binding or packing. I can throw my voice into the masculine vocal range at will.

One distinct experience was from a time approximately one year prior to my "real-life test." At the time, I identified publicly as a stone soft butch. I had found drag king shows a socially acceptable way to pack and bind, to see if I was comfortable in my male skin.

A lesbian in the LGBTQ community told me after a performance, "Don't be a man. You aren't a man, just a stone diesel dyke." It hurt me deeply. It was the one community that had seemed to accept me as me, and suddenly I was met with discrimination again. It became the day I learned transphobia exists in all communities—the day I began to distance myself from that community.

When I stepped back from the trans community in Washington DC, it was because I was having difficulty taking my own advice. I repeatedly told people that operation status doesn't change anything—your gender isn't your sex. I spent a few years depressed because I felt like a fraud for even considering birthing bio children while also considering transition. Something I would *never* chide someone else for, which was internalized ableism and self-gaslighting.

Almost 15 years later, I am still not a female in gender, though I do have some feminine qualities. Yet I have come to a sort of grudging acceptance of my physical body to meet those goals—and I have two more young children. Now that I no longer wish to have more children at 43, top surgery is back on the table again.

Bottom surgery? Maybe. Not because I no longer feel male, but because even with surgical advances, I have a real problem with there not being the technology and ability to have a natural erection.

So to the question... Am I happy? Yes and no. I am accepting of where I am on my trans journey. I am happy with my family, but I wish

I had my dick. My breasts are simply an anatomical feeding device... And if they disappeared overnight, I would be ecstatic, just as soon as our youngest baby weans.

So how does this all mesh with being autistic and that lived experience?

At this time I am currently self- and peer-diagnosed with formal support of that diagnosis from medical professionals, until ADOS testing is completed to officially document the diagnosis. I have had so many hurdles being identified and have been so grateful for my experiences and validation by other autistic people, both formally and informally diagnosed.

At a very young age, it was noted that I was hyperlexic. My first spoken words were one day after my first birthday—and in full sentences. My speech patterns were always noted to be pedantic and more formal than required of my age. My parents divorced when I was very young, which led to other problems. The family I was raised with had abuse problems, a "suck it up" approach, and a "We don't need people in our family's business" mentality. Looking back now, I see where this created more challenges.

I was identified as highly gifted very early in my academic career. My lack of social skills meant that I was not grade accelerated. Being the runt in my family, I was often bullied and beaten by siblings. I learned to mask at an extremely young age as a matter of survival. I rarely acted up in school for many years because I was more afraid of the consequences at home. Let's call it applied behavior analysis at home with no guidance. It wasn't, but the result was the same: extensive masking, trauma, physical or emotional abuse to stop stims and gender expression, and serious bouts of gaslighting. My first diagnosed "stress" ulcer was at age 12.

At 14, I switched living arrangements to my other parent. Within a few short months, my behaviors got me institutionalized and labeled bipolar. The irony was that the doctor stated I was mostly manic and super-fast cycling. No one picked up that my "depressive episodes" were actually trauma-induced depression with near instantaneous masking. Almost three years later, after a lot of unnecessary and even abusive therapies, I was released into foster care until I was of age. I was finally diagnosed as having attention deficit hyperactivity disorder (ADHD) and not bipolar disorder. My social skills issues were still considered part of my trauma; my gender expression just a weird phase. My now quite evident problems in school were supposedly because I was "emotionally disabled" and had a learning disability. Yes, even at the school in the institution, but more so in high school senior year. My individual education plan took away the one thing I was passionate about: an automotive vocational technology curriculum that was replaced despite my protests with a basic skills class that was essentially a waste of time study hall.

My "special interests" were considered normal tomboy crap, even though I did things like became a walk-on for varsity wrestling. If I had a serious interest in anything, it was called ADHD hyperfocus.

I did my best to fight for my needs. And was turned down. Every. Single. Time. "Kids don't know what they need."

My hearing problems were dismissed. Tests came back normal. I have since learned it isn't a hearing deficit, but a processing delay. I have similar vision processing issues and as part of my evaluation, we may also find I am dyslexic. Another commonality.

I honestly did not even know autism existed outside the movie *Rain Man* until one of my children was going through the diagnostic process.

And yet, going through that process for one of my children, which started as speech evaluation, we learned more and more as a family. As an individual, my ability to hyperfocus went into overdrive. At first, most of what I could find was from resources like Autism Speaks and Talk About Curing Autism, two resources I now shoo people away from with fervor. I have become a neurodiversity advocate in the two-and-a-half years down this path since. Not one professional who has met me since has said I am not autistic.

I still sometimes doubt the veracity of my own acceptance of my autistic identity. The amount of gaslighting experienced as a child and young adult have made it almost second nature to do to myself. It is a hard road to travel. I am constantly plagued by the "what ifs." What if I am making stuff up? What if I just should accept I am bipolar (regardless of it being removed as a faulty diagnosis)? What if I am just trying to be a "special snowflake"? What if the doctors evaluate me and say I am just an anxious trans person still dealing with unresolved trauma? What if all my investigations, quizzes, self-administered diagnostic tools, readings, and confirmation by fellow Autists is all...wrong? What if I am just a fraud?

I know I am not a fraud. Not as an autistic person or a transgender person. Without a doubt. However, the extent of perpetual harm that systemic gaslighting and dismissal do is much more horrendous than many people realize.

So, I advocate. With individuals in my community, as an administrator of a neurodiversity-promoting Facebook group. Within my own family. I fight, and I fight hard because it should not be this difficult. I should not get raised eyebrows from others for wearing sunglasses indoors due to bright lights. I should not have to fight to have music turned down. I should not have to ignore people who question my choice of restroom. I should not have to seek out "family" restrooms to avoid confrontations. I should not have to argue about not being able to beat the autism out of my kid. I should not have to say, "They tried with me, but they couldn't beat the autism out of me." I should not have to dumb myself down to be taken seriously. I should not have to hear "You are too high functioning to be autistic" by parents of autistic kids simply for advocating. Just. Stop.

In summary, what does it mean to be transtistic?

It means that I think on a Linux-style operating system as opposed to Windows or MacOS, with a physical shape that does not equate to my vision of myself. It isn't body dysphoria in the traditional, clinical sense. It is some warped concept that I must be a square. I have to be a square. And yet, I still have four sides. They are still the same length. I am...a rhombus trapped in a rectangle because people are still trying to fix me by adding two triangles on each side to make a square—so that it can then be morphed to convince me that I am only a rectangle, not a square, and much less a rhombus. Because rhombi are special. And rare. And apparently defunct with no real use to the world.

I reject that hypothesis. And I will continue to fight until rhombi are accepted as an alternative leaning square. No better, no worse, just much more beautiful.

_____

*Jordan is a 43-year-old neurodiversity advocate raising a family in a non-traditional manner. They enjoy billiards, needle felting, and other flights of fancy.*

# My Path of Life

*Elie B (they/them/their)*

As I try to organize my thoughts to write, I find them cluttered and entangled in emotions. Reflecting on my life as an autistic trans person, reliving specific scenes, I can still feel anger, anguish, and some form of shame.

I was born in 1989 in France, assigned a girl at birth. When my mother first saw me, she was surprised by this serious "boyish" looking baby. When she put me in day care, she was told I had a "strange gaze" and I stayed away from the other children; also, when I was angry, I would bang my head on the floor. But I learned to talk very quickly, I smiled, and in school I made a good friend, so everything seemed fine.

In secondary school, I was severely bullied by other students, who thought I was wrong in the head. They would physically hurt me, and I'd stay mute. I started feeling really bad, fostering aggressive thoughts and considering self-harm. In my first year of high school, in November, I brought in a knife. I didn't harm anyone, but I was kicked out and sent to a psychiatric day hospital.

I saw a lot of shrinks. None of them gave me a solid diagnosis, except a "delirious breath" (a sudden and momentary onset of delusional episodes in a person who previously didn't have any visible problems) for taking a weapon into school. As I needed to understand my differences, I started looking for an explanation myself. When I came across Asperger's syndrome, I finally recognized my lack of social abilities, my sensory issues, and all my "weird" behavior.

I left the psychiatric day hospital when I got my bachelor's degree. I still saw a psychologist from there, who was also a psychoanalyst. He said the knife was a phallic substitute and that I unconsciously wanted to sexually penetrate my bully—no wonder I had regular joyful dreams about growing a penis. I suppose that psychologist was very into Freud.

When I told him about Asperger's syndrome, he laughed at me. He thought I had problems because of "my path of life." He admitted that maybe I had a "developmental psychotic disharmony." Googling this strange combination of words, I realized how behind France was in accepting recent research on autism.

I stopped seeing him and started working for the cause. I became a translator of American courses on applied behavior analysis, an assistant for a film called *The Wall* or *psychoanalysis put to the test of autism*, and a caregiver for a teen with autism, supervised by his mother who had to become a behavior analyst herself so that her son would have a chance of autonomy in this society.

In the meantime, I had made a request to a specialized autism diagnosis center. I got an appointment more than a year later. I passed a lot of tests. The woman in charge told me that I had all the criteria, but she felt that I wasn't an aspie. She said, "A high IQ with a certain path of life can resemble autism."

I think what they call my "path of life" is the abuse from neurotypical people. I think maybe it wouldn't have been so bad if I had been recognized early as an aspie, if I had received proper social education, if my schoolmates were less ignorant about it, and if the adults around us were more aware of the risks. It makes me very angry.

But at least by calling myself an autistic person despite all of this, I learned to define myself without the validation of others, especially without the validation of so-called experts.

So this helped me to get rid of the "girl" label. It took a few years, but I finally decided to take testosterone. I had always identified more with boys, I had always hated my high voice and my figure. I had never stuck to gender stereotypes, one way or another—they just seem absurd and harmful.

It was still hard to come out, because I was raised with a certain type of feminism: the only distinction between men and women was their sex. My mother had true noble intentions. I could do anything, I could love anything, I could be anything—but always as a girl.

My need to transition became undeniable when I became pregnant. Reflections on the sex of the child, how I didn't want to display it because of the projections of others, how I chose a unisex name with the father; being seen more as a woman than ever, and feeling so wrong about it although I wanted the child very much, all that was finally enough to overcome my resistance to change.

I started seeking professional help about my gender transition when I was seven months pregnant. I went to a trans association. It was so hard to join a group. One group member said I was "just a poor lost little cis girl." I found that very inappropriate and knew I wouldn't find support there. But it didn't stop me.

I went to an endocrinologist, and she was stunned. I told her, of course, that I would only take the testosterone after my child was born. Still, I didn't seem trans enough for her, as I walked in with my big belly and boobs. I told her that I didn't identify as the stereotypical manly man either, that I had always been out of the binary, and that my needs were real and important.

She told me they didn't make freaks here, like bearded women in the circus. I said some people were actually born that way, and they weren't freaks. She told me intersex people were mistakes that should be corrected. I said this was abuse, and our country had been condemned for mutilations on intersex people several times, and then I left. I was very much autistic—zero tact and zero flexibility regarding moral views. I do not regret it.

I had my child, my lovely Alex. I wasn't surprised when I saw the signs. Even the father is not the most neurotypical guy. In day care, they told us that Alex might be deaf. She was not, even though she didn't speak. I voiced my concerns, but people were very doubtful, as always: they saw a happy, engaging child! They didn't know how much work and effort I put into the way I interacted with Alex, to teach them the most basic social things, like manding, that didn't come spontaneously.

Without too much hope, I took my child to a diagnosis center, not saying anything about my own opinion. And they did diagnose Alex with typical autism. What a relief, this time. My child now has their needs properly addressed and is making huge progress.

Anyway, after the pregnancy, once my body was ready, I found that if I wanted testosterone, I still had to find a way to avoid gatekeeping. I had to lie. I reconnected with the trans community, but online, with selected people. Thanks to them, I found the address of an endocrinologist known to give the prescription without too many questions, on the first appointment, as long as you had a certificate from a psychiatrist. Fortunately, I went to one good psychiatrist—they do exist—who wrote me a letter basically stating I was mentally healthy and capable of informed consent regarding my body and identity.

The first shot was so nice. And the next one. And the next one. Two years on, I have had the boobs removed and changed my name, and I've never been more myself. A non-binary, autistic person, defined by themself. Now that is my path of life.

---

*Elie is a French author, of mostly thrillers. They like chilling in their apartment, drinking cocoa, and watching movies, when they're not playing outside with their very energetic child.*

# Autistic, Non-binary, and Still Learning

*Alyssa Hillary (they/them/their)*

When I was younger, people thought I was a cute (if weird) little girl. They were right about the "weird" part, though that wasn't the whole story, and wrong about the "girl" part. I'm autistic, and I'm transgender—specifically non-binary, and more specifically wandering between autism either being a gender or occupying the place gender would normally go, not having a gender at all, and being somewhat androgynous. So even though I am genderfluid, I don't expect that to be relevant to most people—non-binary always works for me.

As time has gone on, some people have learned more about who I really am. In graduate school, just about everyone knows I'm autistic. A bright orange Autistic Party Giraffe shirt is hard for most sighted people to miss, after all, and the times I type or write instead of talking tend to give me away too. I don't know how many people understand what it means when I tell them I'm non-binary, but it's not a secret. There's a "they/them" pronoun pin on my jacket as I write this.

They don't know everything about who I am, of course, or all the details of what it means to be autistic and non-binary. They're still learning. Here's the thing: so am I. I am still learning, and I am still changing, and I expect to be doing so for as long as I live. Identity is complicated. For one version of the short list of my identities, because let's be real, I probably couldn't make a complete list if I tried and it might well change tomorrow anyway, I am:

- autistic
- an autism researcher
- an agnostic Jew
- non-binary
- a mathematician
- a neuroscientist
- a writer
- asexual
- a disability studies scholar
- a teacher
- panromantic
- a part-time AAC (augmentative and alternative communication) user
- an AAC researcher
- a graduate student.

I am always all of these things, and more. But some of these identities are consistently tied together. When we're talking autism, both my autism research and my status as an autistic person are relevant, and the combination is especially relevant. And at any given time, some of my identities may be more relevant than others. When I'm presenting or writing, literally anywhere that asks me for a short introduction, my being non-binary is important: I am a they, and sometimes people notice. But when I teach online, the fact that I'm a part-time user of augmentative and alternative communication may not matter much.

Nowadays, I think about how these identities combine fairly frequently. I'm an AAC user, I do AAC research, I took a class on AAC, and I went back to give a talk for the next year's students in the same AAC class I took. Am I the curriculum? Am I a teacher? Am I a student? Am I a researcher? Yes.

But it's being both queer and autistic where I started thinking this way. It's being queer and autistic, being transgender and autistic, being asexual and non-binary and autistic, where I started needing to think about all this, where I started learning in public about all this. I threw together an abstract about the erasure of queer autistic people in Washington DC, over what I think was winter break in 2013.[50]

Looking back at this work, I don't think I really knew what I was doing. I know there were things I wanted to discuss that I had to leave out, because I wasn't sure how to explain them then. I wanted to talk about how even the use of "crip" in Crip Theory as the intersection of disability and queerness could be exclusionary for those of us whom crip was never about. At the conference, I even did. An audience member asked if using crip would then be erasing themselves. I don't remember what I said in response. Heck, I don't even remember if I said anything in response! Robert McRuer, the author of Crip Theory, was in the audience, and he kind of answered the question for me. He talked about how "crip" could be a stretchy word. I don't disagree that it can stretch. I don't think my neurodivergent friends who refer to Crip Theory are erasing themselves.

But...why are the terms that stretch beyond their domains the ones from physical disability? Sure, "mad" stretches some, but I've only ever seen it used for things that are either mental or mistaken for mental. It's physical disability terms that are expected to stretch for everyone.

I won't argue with the neurodivergent people, with the mad people, who stretch physical disability words to claim them. Heck, the essay I eventually published is in *Criptiques*, of all places. I wonder if that's part of why musings on "crip" not really being mine and the expectation that physical disability words stretch for everyone didn't make it into my final draft. I felt no great need to exclude myself from a place that would have me, even if their words aren't really mine. And they aren't really mine. They were never mine. "Crip theory" is not mine. "Disability communities are not mine."[51]

> You know, they told me, I don't look... Nobody would have to... I could be just another crip.
>
> And as if I were just another crip, they started with the jokes and comebacks.
>
> "She asked me whether my toenails still grow; I asked her whether her hair still grows."
>
> "They want cognitive disability representation? Why don't they just ask 'SuperChris': he's cognitively disabled."
>
> "They may be able-bodied, but we're able-minded."
>
> They didn't mean me, of course. I wasn't like that, wasn't like them. They meant no offense. Perhaps it is enough to say that my vision of "the disability community" and theirs don't coincide.[52]

I didn't include that quote in the end, either, but it was in my mind as I worked. Because I knew, and I still know. Crip isn't mine. I could try to stretch it, but it's not my word. I think my mind is fine, because I think all minds are fine, but I know I'm not what physical disability community people mean when they say their minds are fine.

But I am transgender and I am disabled. Specifically, I am autistic and non-binary.

Where do I fit?

Do I fit?

What is community?

I am, again, still learning. I don't know where I fit yet, if I fit. Here, perhaps, where we're all transgender and autistic. Here is nice. It isn't enough. And I'm still trying to figure it all out. What will I wish I'd said, six years from now?

This is the point where I point to the *Talmud*. Agnostic Jew, remember? Depending on the translation, Rabbi Tarfon says it is not up to me to finish the work, or I'm not obligated to complete it, but I am not free to abandon it or to desist. The context was Torah study, but I think it applies here. I am not obligated to know everything about the combination of being transgender and autistic. It wouldn't be possible. But, especially if I'm going to claim to be a person who knows things about it, I've got to keep thinking and learning and growing. I don't get to abandon the work.

And I do claim to be a person who knows things about this. Writing here is a claim that I know things about being transgender and autistic. Writing for *Challenging Genders*[53] was a claim that I know things about being non-binary, designated female at birth, and because of what I wrote there, autistic. Presenting and writing about "The Erasure of Queer Autistic People" for a conference and then for *Criptiques*[54] was a claim that I know things about being queer (non-binary, panromantic, asexual in my case) and autistic. And that was the start of my truly academic writing, not something I'm ever really leaving behind. Reading all about the experiences of other people like me, finding themes in them, and connecting the lot to existing scholarship taught me how to do so.

But it wasn't just about learning how to write academically. Writing "The Erasure of Queer Autistic People" taught me to think critically about my connection to my work:

> Writing this, I realized: Why do I feel the need, writing academically, to distance myself from my identities? Why is this expected in academia? So I won't do so. I say "we," not "they" for groups I am a member of. I will not feign the distanced impartiality of an outside observer: it would be erasing my own Queer Autistic voice to do so![55]

I told readers, right at the start, that I was writing about the erasure of queer autistic people as a queer autistic person. Because I was. I didn't, however, tell my readers that I was genderfluid, moving between a bunch of different genders that are all non-binary. I knew I was non-binary. I just didn't specify, and I feel like maybe I should have. I'm not sure. Was it better to leave it at "queer" to describe myself, or would it have been better to say, yes, I'm non-binary, and I'm asexual, and I'm either biromantic or panromantic, and as long as you're using non-transphobic definitions, either of those will fit? That's one bit I still don't know.

At that point, I hadn't publicly changed my pronouns to they/them/theirs. So at that time, writing "they" was only dis-identification: whoever I write "they" about is not me. Writing about a group I'm part of, that would make "they" erasure. Now, it's a bit more complicated.

Were I to say "they" about queer autistic people as a whole, it would still be pretending not to be who I am. It would still be erasure. But.

I am non-binary. My correct pronouns are they/them/theirs. The "they" in my byline tells you who I am: a non-binary person who uses they/them pronouns. Which makes "they" an act of asserting my identity. If I write "they" about myself and "they" about a group like queer autistic people or autistic AAC users, I'm still using the same pronoun for both myself and the group. Would it change the distancing effect of calling my community "they" to call myself "they" as well?

It's not enough for me to do it in a piece about being my being trans and autistic, and not enough for me to do it in a piece about being an autistic AAC user, but enough for me to call autistic AAC users "they" when I'm intentionally not discussing my own experiences with AAC. It makes me feel better about it, at least. Being a writer is hard.

And, as I expect many writers understand, part of me wishes I had a time machine. Can I go back and edit my essays with everything I know now, like Diane Duane got to do with her *Young Wizards*[56] series? I know more now. Lots of people know more now. Some of the studies I'd loved to have cited when saying, actually, who there are a lot of us didn't exist then. Especially on the transgender side of things—I'd have loved to have cited "'I Don't Feel Like a Gender, I Feel Like Myself': Autistic Individuals Raised as Girls Exploring Gender Identity"[57] way back then, but it's only been very recently published. People are doing the work, and I love it, and I wish I knew about it, had it to point to, before it even existed.

So can I have a time machine, please?

No?

Can I have one six years from now? In 2013, I wanted to talk more than I did about the sexism in Simon Baron-Cohen's extreme male brain theory and how that's a massive problem for transgender autistic people of any gender. In fairness, I'm still not certain how to word that one, which is why I want a time machine in the further future, when I've maybe managed to figure it out. Because seriously, what is it with this guy and autism theories that do all kinds of damage to transgender autistic people? Theory of mind gets used to say we can't understand what it's like to be ourselves, and that would totally prevent us from recognizing our genders, if the whole idea weren't bullshit.

I've got to do that part. And keep doing that part. Because I didn't know Wenn Lawson[58] was a transgender man when I read and cited his book on sex, sexuality, and the autism spectrum. In my defense, web.archive.org tells me he hadn't updated his site to reflect that yet when I was writing. But I know he's a man now, and that changes my interpretation of some of his writing:

> It was OK for a while because I didn't have the right name for who I was. I conformed to the label I'd been landed with, even though it was very uncomfortable. But, once reality set in and I knew the truth, I could no longer hide behind the make-believe set-up I'd grown up in and adopted as "my life."[59]

This now has additional meaning. He needed, at one point, the word lesbian, in order to know he could like women...but he also needed to know that being a trans man was an option. When he wrote *Sex, Sexuality, and the Autism Spectrum*, Wenn wrote about feeling more male than female and how he eventually accepted being a woman who felt that way. My concern at the time had been that his statement could affect transgender autistic people who would prefer to transition. Which, in fairness, the idea behind it clearly did affect a transgender autistic person: Dr. Wenn Lawson himself. And I was afraid it could affect me: I've since corrected my pronouns everywhere I can, outed myself to my graduate program, and got a proper binder, but I hadn't done any of that when I was reading and writing in 2013.

Knowing that Dr. Lawson really is a man makes me see his statement about accepting womanhood in a different light. I wonder what made him accept, even temporarily, his supposed womanhood after desiring gender confirmation surgery. Was there a fear about being considered too complicated, of being different in too many ways? I've struggled with that one. Was it the barriers we face in transition? Was it his marriage to a woman, made while his wife believed him to be a woman as well? I don't know. (I'm not even really sure it's my business, though some of those questions might be addressed in his later book, *Transitioning Together: One Couple's Journey of Gender and Identity Discovery.*[60] I want to read that, when I have the chance.)

Not that my old concern is totally gone, of course. Even without citing Wenn's older statement, people make the argument that this is an autism thing, that this has something to do with the extreme male brain theory, and that it's totally fine to enforce gender-normativity on us because we just don't socially "get" how gender works. In fairness, I don't totally get gender. Neither do the people claiming I don't understand gender.

So, no, it's not fine to enforce gender roles on us with the assumption that we don't understand them. And if gender and sexual identity are too complex to address well (which people claim, sometimes saying it's especially too complex for us), that doesn't make okay to address it badly. Or are queer autistic people supposed to be too complex for ourselves? Does the fact that I am, in fact, confused about gender mean that my transgender identity doesn't get to be real? Or is it your confusion about my gender that's really the problem here?

Yes, gender is complicated. Yes, it confuses me. I still needed to be told enough about gender to know that "none of the above" was an option.

"Hey, gender is complicated, you might not (ever) totally get it, and it's okay to explore gender as part of understanding it better rather than waiting for certainty that might not ever come" is a thing it's possible to say! In fact, if I had to turn my thoughts on gender into an elevator pitch on a day when speech was mostly working, I'd probably say something like that. Identity is complicated. Explore. It's okay to still be learning.

---

*Alyssa Hillary is an autistic non-binary graduate student in neuroscience who uses AAC part time. They've written about some of those things before, too.*

## RECOMMENDED READING

Egner, J.E. (2018) "'The disability rights community was never mine:' Neuroqueer disidentification." *Gender & Society.* 33(1), 123–147.

Hillary, A. (under review) "Am I the curriculum?" Submitted to Curriculum Inquiry.

Zisk, A.H. & Dalton, E. (in press) "Augmentative and Alternative Communication for Speaking Autistic Adults: Overview and Recommendations." Accepted at *Autism in Adulthood.*

# Remember the Time

V. Mike Roberts (he/him/his)

One day, when I was six, I went out for recess. Well, okay, there was more than one day like that, but there was one particular day that I remember extremely well—I saw an adult behaving oddly. The adult was watching a big kid playing in the sand. The kid was copying patterns. The drawing was a little bit different each time, but not very different. That was interesting, so I went over to the kid and said hello. He didn't tell me to go away, so I didn't. I remember noticing that the adult who had been over there (leaning on the red brick of the building) kind of startled, and made a beeline towards us. The adult told me the that the other kid didn't want to play with me. I told the adult that the kid hadn't said to go away. The adult told me to go play with something else. I said no. The adult told me the other kids were doing something (or something to that effect—in any case, none of these quotes are exactly accurate). I ignored him. The adult asked me if I wanted to play with him. I said no, and that I was having fun.

This whole time, the other kid had kept on doing what he was doing. I must have asked him something, because the adult answered...

"He can't talk, he's autistic," the adult told me. Now, this is where the memory becomes extremely clear. I remember looking at the adult as if he had three heads. I did this because I thought that the adult was insane. I did not understand why this ridiculous creature was bothering me, or the other boy, for that matter. After a glare of substantial length (something I often got in trouble for doing at the time) and some consideration, I informed the adult that the kid was not artistic, he was just doing patterns, that there was nothing wrong with that, and that I did not care if the other kid talked to me, he clearly didn't mind my watching.

At this point, there ensued a very long discussion between the adult and me, during which we discussed elocution, the letter r, the meaning of art, the difference between practicing artistic skills and actually doing art, the word "autism," and what autism was. I was having none of it. The word was "artistic," I knew exactly what it meant, and my definitions of art were distinctly clearer and more comprehensive than the adult's, so even if I were making errors, he was clearly making more errors. His description of "autism" made no sense, and therefore could not be a real thing. The kid was fine, there was nothing wrong with him, and I wanted to hang out with him.[61] Please stop bothering us. The adult, who I remember looked thoroughly confused, kinda just watched us until the other kid got up and went to class. I didn't say bye, because he didn't, but I remember being worried the adult would get me into trouble for that. At that point, though, I was much too angry at the adult to hedge my bets.

I don't remember being angry very much as a child. I did find it very hard to pretend to agree with people. Even at that age, I was well aware that the main thing that went wrong when I was angry was that I became too honest and too authentic. I said things that were true, but that people didn't want to hear. They would then tell me I didn't really mean it, and that would make me more angry, because if I was sure of anything, it was that I really meant whatever it was.

In retrospect, knowing that the worst thing I could do at the age of six was to be honest and authentically myself was likely somewhat damaging. Even today, as I write this, I flip back and forth between my authentic voice, and one produced for consumption. I consider it a strength that I can balance authenticity with palatability. Palatability is the first and the last pass when I edit my work. In this text, I have included some of my autism in the endnotes, as a way of presenting a more authentic voice, while remaining palatable in the main text.[62]

In retrospect, the other kid must have thrown a tantrum and refused to go inside. The school had a wing where there were behavioral and autism spectrum disorder (ASD) classrooms. Those students had recess and lunch times at different times from the "regular" kids, and we were not supposed to meet or interact. The wing was mysterious, and some people said it was abandoned; there were even ghost stories that circulated among the students. Holding was a regular feature of intervention for the autistic kids so unless this boy had been very hard to contain, he would not have been left outside at the start of "our" recess...but by the time I saw him, he had clearly cooled down. The adult must have been afraid I would get hurt, so that's probably why he started towards us with such a lurch, and probably why he was smoking and lounging by the wall while on duty. He was probably doing self-care, cooling himself down so he could handle the kid.

A while later, I was invited to volunteer in the autism classroom. I found this very exciting for a number of reasons, including my genuine desire to save the world and my genuine interest in the kid. I was enthusiastic, and on my best behavior...and there were some problems...but I resolved not to care. I desperately wanted to be there, and in my six-year-old mind, it felt like a calling.

The first problem was the smell. The ASD kids got hot lunches, and that food smelled terrible.[63] It was hard not to gag as one approached the classrooms. As soon as one passed the fire-doors,[64] which separated the behavioral wing from the rest of the school, the smell accosted you. I remember that the paint and lighting on the other side of those doors were also somewhat different. The memories now play like a creepy scene, but a creepy scene in a fairly up-beat TV show, something like *Star Trek*. It felt off, but not off like in a horror movie. It was not blood-curdling wrong, just nauseating.

The second problem was the hooting and the banging. There were about eight kids in the room, and at least half of them were fairly continuously stimming. One particular kid had a kind of a hooting that will be familiar to anyone who has spent time with lots of autistic people. Even I make that noise when I'm alone and I think no one can hear me, but hearing it is not the same as making it. He really never stopped, either, and it became like a disconcerting wallpaper. You forgot you were hearing it, but your muscles still stayed tensed. Sometimes, while I was talking to him he would kind of stop, but not for very long. The banging came mainly from the fact that there was pretty much always someone angry enough to throw or hit things. It wasn't continuous, but it was close.

Aside from those problems, I loved it. The kids did really cool stuff and my job was to sit with them and be interested in what they were doing. I buckled down and endured the smell and the noise and the dark,[65] and I acted as if I was okay. I tried not to be rude when they offered me lunch, and I always asked when could I come back. I think I kept going for about two weeks, but finally, the environment was too much. I remember asking if I could be with the kids, but outdoors. I never really got an answer, but no one ever came to get me again. I was ready every day for a long time. I couldn't tell you if it was weeks or months, but suffice it to say, I was disappointed and I thought I must have done something wrong. I was very poor at labeling my feelings in those days, but I physicalize my feeling very strongly, and I remember the sensation. When my father died, I recognized that one as grief.

About ten years later, during a full psychoeducational work-up, all my many, many[66] scales came back saying I was autistic. The consultant in the room literally laughed that off, and I remember my mother and her making jokes and guffawing (really shrilly, like they were scared and trying to cover it up). I remember thinking they were being awfully nasty about autistic people, but I can't remember what they said, except one thing: that I couldn't be autistic because autistic people can't talk. I'd known that I was autistic since those couple of weeks in the ASD classroom, and I'd known quite clearly since my friend D.K. had introduced me to the internet.[67] But that awkward experience, at the age of 17, was when I knew for sure that I was autistic.

Some of my memories are very early—early enough that once I learned a bit about how cognition develops, I realized I could sometimes date them by what I was able to perceive at the time. Time itself is very distorted in most of the early ones, but feelings of identity are actually more coherent the further back I think. This is where we get to the question of gender. I do not remember being two years old and thinking, "I'm a boy!" What I do remember is being two years old and swinging on a railing in a pool and feeling in accord with myself. I physicalize my feelings, and I remember the sensations quite clearly, even for feelings I had no words for at the time I made the memory. Swinging on that railing I had several sensations which I still have no words for...

The first is a feeling of smoothness. A feeling that I am acting without editing my actions, and no one is objecting. I'm not in trouble, even though I'm being authentic.

The second is the feeling of being in accord with myself. Sometimes, when one strives for something, if feels like work, but other times when one strives for something it feels right and good and warming. That second feeling, when you are pushing yourself but it feels good and invigorating, is what I mean by feeling in accord.

Third is a sort of gravitational pull we feel when we aspire to be more like someone we respect and identify with. In these early memories, that pull is often prominent. I knew who I aspired to be like, and I knew in what ways I aspired to be like them.

When I remember swinging on that railing, I remember feeling like if I kept doing this, I would be more like the boys.[68] I remember feeling that aspiration as being in accord, and I remember that feeling of smoothness. Together, those things make this memory a favorite. I found a photograph of me on that railing when I was in my 20s. My father remembered that someone had been worried about me getting hurt but that they'd let me do it anyway. He remembered that he'd never seen me have so much fun but he was really surprised I remembered it. It turns out that the pool was in Florida, where I did not live, which is why I could never find the pool again. My father was shocked when I told him that I hadn't given up on looking for it until well into my teens, but he did remember me asking about it at least for a few weeks.

There's one more piece I haven't said yet, though. That feeling of smoothness—of being authentic but not getting into trouble—is the most strongly marked sensation in the memory. At the time, I was surprised I wasn't getting into trouble, and I was waiting for my luck to break. At two years old, when three-word sentences were all the rage and I barely had words for snacks, let alone for gender transgression, I was already conscious of being trans. I knew people didn't like it when I strove to be more like the boys, but I also knew that striving that way felt good to me. There is another sensation in the memory, and that is the pleasure of solitude. A feeling of relief that no one seemed to be watching me. I felt free, because no one was there to stop me from being authentically me. That's a lot of distrust and discomfort directed at strangers, day-care staff, and my parents. Most two-year-olds don't like being lost.

The concept of this anthology seems to demand an answer to the question "Is there a connection between transness and autism?" My answer is "I'm not sure." Of course there is a connection between my transness and my autism, and people have a certain fundamental integrity; no matter how complex or alien a lived experience might seem, we are each—literally—a unified being. Everything about us is by definition part of one thing. My autism and my transness interact not because of some theoretical linkage between them, like the throttle linkage on a car, but because they are both the same stuff. They are both me, like a part name and a part number, they describe the same object. It's best not to confuse the two when you place a big order, but that doesn't mean they don't describe the same thing! Our society isn't really into that idea, though, and over the years I've learned to separate them out, talk about only one, or only the other, because if you've got too much going on it's probably just that you want attention. You couldn't be that weird organically, could you? If your child is autistic, it's best to avoid talking about how you are as well, or they will think you are just projecting. If your son wears long hair, and they know you are trans, they will decide he must be trans because you taught him to be. It's better to avoid these things. Especially when children are involved, it's flat out unsafe to risk these things.

The problem with the habit, however, is that the lessons about gender that can be found in my autistic memory, with its tendency to encode weird specifics and nameless ideas, are lost. Ellen Lewin askes us explicitly: "how many identities can each of us possess, and how much variation can we accommodate before the boundaries of identities begin to crumble?"[69] My answer is a resounding "All of them." We can possess all of our identities. And we must.

---

*V. Mike Roberts is a "mature" student who enjoys archaeology, history, and arguing about philosophical matters at otherwise polite events.*

# a letter to a friend

*ren koloni (they/them/their or it/it/its)*

friend of mine, i want to tell you who you can be.

i want to tell you that you can be autistic. if the dance of a candle is music to your eyes, if you pull a heavy blanket over your shoulders and feel peace, if you settle into your special interest and relief and joy and brightness wash over you like cool water, you can be autistic.

there is no test to pass or fail; there is no magical questionnaire for you and your mother to both take at the same time; there is no signed form that will unlock a door. there is only you, and you can be autistic.

and i want to tell you that you can be trans. if the way they tell you to wear your hair doesn't weigh right on your head, if the clothes they give you scratch and pull at your body in the mirror and threaten to tell the whole world that you are someone you are not, if they ask what you are and you know there is not a spoken word in the world that could tell them, you can be trans.

you do not need to hate your hips (but if you do, i understand). you do not need to change your body (but if you do, it will be beautiful). you do not need to change your pronouns or your name (but if you do, they will be yours).

if it helps you, if it makes sense to you, if it clicks in your mind, you can be these things. they are for you.

\*

friend of mine, i want to tell you what i am.

when they ask me, are you a boy or a girl? i say "i am not" but this is what i mean.

i am the tips of my fingers dragging through the tickling ends of tall grass.

i am the feeling of pulling on a big hoodie, safe and spacious, the warmth humming on my skin.

i am the clarity of a soft clear sea washing over sand.

i am the soft blurred glow of a lamppost on a foggy night.

i am the sheen on a grackle's feather, or the lines of light on a labradorite you twist and turn in the light.

i am my hair, cut just the way i want it, soft and puffing up at the ends, haloing my face, something to pull or stroke or shake.

i am my voice, deep and melodious. i am my hands in motion, flapping and slapping and twisting and singing. i am a sunset through the window, clouds settling over trees, light sighing into darkness.

i am all these things and more, and maybe you are too.

*

friend of mine, i want to tell you that you do not have to know what your gender is.

"man" and "woman" don't have to make sense to you. even new words, the ones we made to make sense to more of us, like "demigirl" or "autigender" or "bigender" or "neutrois," don't have to make sense to you.

you don't have to know what you like to be called, or what you like to wear, or what you like your body to feel like. gender is a journey, and you don't have to know where you're going to end up.

if you're lost, find yourself in the little things. (like we autistics always do.)

i like longer hair because i can tie it back and wrap it around my hands and feel its comfortable weight.

i like to push my hands under my breasts, big and warm, and feel the weight shift and bounce.

i want people to look at my face and have to look again because they aren't sure what they saw.

the first time someone asked me if i was a boy or a girl i wondered if they could see the way my lungs lit up like fireflies, happy and bright.

*

friend of mine, i want to tell you that you do not have to make sense to other people.

if you're safe, if you're comfortable, if you want, you can tell people what you are, or what you want to be, or what makes you light up. but all of those things are for you—never for them.

it is a privilege for someone to know you in your entirety. you get to decide who has that privilege.

*

friend of mine, i want to tell you that they cannot keep us down.

they can try to stop us flapping and humming and feeling and being, but they can't. they won't.

they can try to stop us from learning who we are or being who we are, but they can't. they won't.

they cannot stop us from being loud.

friend of mine, i am here, too. i am flapping and humming and feeling and being. i am learning who i am, i am being who i am, i am being loud and bright and joyful and true!

and they are afraid, and they do not understand, but i am not for them

and friend of mine, neither are you.

---

*ren is a disabled, queer, non-binary autistic person from virginia. they like to talk and think about disability, gender, and trauma, and also video games.*

# Gender Epiphany

*Eryn Star (Any pronouns. I highly encourage folks to call*
*me different pronouns interchangeably, but if someone is*
*unable to due to disability reasons, they/them is good.)*

I can't get enough of running my hands through the long, dark hair
on my armpits and my legs. My leg hair is much smoother than I
expected it to be, and I love the way my armpit hair curls at the ends.
Leaving my body unshaved and unwaxed has freed me from pain
and given me autonomy. I feel a blend of feminine and masculine,
an expression that's *me*.

For about a year, I had this recurring fantasy of me performing as
a drag king in front of a cheering audience. I would be wearing a suit
jacket and flowing floral pants, my hair in a cascade of wavy curls.
Then in my first year of college, I told one of my friends about it and
they told me I should do the annual drag show. At first, I hesitated
because I didn't believe I had the resources, skill, and talent I thought
was required. However, the possibility of fulfilling my dream was
impossible to resist. I named my drag king persona David Wilde after
David Bowie and Oscar Wilde and I based my look and personality on
a combination of them. I put my hair in waves and wore red Converse
high-tops, a three-quarter sleeve with ruffle trim, and a floral suit
jacket and pants. When I walked onstage, I felt more empowered
than I ever have before in my life. I was funny, I was flirtatious, I was
powerful, I was gloriously unique. I held the audience in the palm of
my hand from the moment I introduced myself and then lip-synced

to David Bowie's "Let's Dance." In drag space, my body hair is beautiful, my movement is beautiful, I am a delightful surprise, I am filled with self-love. For a long time, I denied how connected David Wilde is to me. I said to people, "He's a character, nothing more." That is 100 percent wrong. David Wilde is a symbol of who I could be one day.

When I got two suit jackets and trousers as birthday presents, I was filled with so much happiness to the point where I thought I was going to burst. I do enjoy my feminine clothes, but I wish for my clothes to reflect a variety of expression. It's interesting how my sensory needs as an autistic person play a role here. I love the feeling of flowing cotton skirts and dresses that billow in the wind and I love a suit jacket with broad shoulders and trousers with a belt. However, it's difficult for me to present as masculine in the summer because I'd be too overwhelmed by the heat. There are days when I want to wear a dress, but it's too cold. I hate shaving because the razor hurts and my legs itch. Every time I get my eyebrows, lip hair, and chin hair waxed, I feel pain so intense that I'm immediately in tears the entire time.

This being called "woman" is quite difficult to be. Woman feels like a weird word to call myself these days; man feels weird as well. Whenever I say "woman" or "man," I feel all this baggage weighing on my head. I see myself as a person and I want others to call me a person instead. When I was asked to list my gender on a form for a program I was traveling to, I started panicking because I don't like being called a woman, but I'm cis, right? So I put in "Cis W," but I still felt anxious. It was when watching a performance of *The Vagina Monologues* that everything hit me. I didn't relate to any of the monologues at all—I felt disconnected from womanhood. I knew that my monologue wouldn't fit in that space. I thought I was a cis woman but my feelings seem to have shifted.

Thinking back now, I've learned that my reaction to hearing the term "non-binary" for the first time may not be a common reaction.

Most people respond, "What?!" When a person I met in high school told me they were non-binary, my response was, "Okay!" Then I went online and researched non-binary gender identities for hours (and have been reading about gender identity most days since). Accepting the existence of this concept that I had just learned about came naturally to me. This person is a person—why would I question who they are? I think being autistic has shaped me into an accepting person. I never resisted rejecting the gender binary. Since accepting the people I love for who they are means expanding my worldview, I shall always look towards learning knowledge, dismantling oppression, and celebrating existence. Once I learn something new about people in my life, I commit what I've learned about them to long-term memory. Because of this, it hasn't been difficult for me to remember someone's gender identity and pronouns. If I wasn't autistic (difficult to imagine a universe where I wouldn't be autistic), perhaps I would have been less accepting. Now, I think my need to learn everything I can about gender has sparked another journey.

I dream of a day when my body is my own. I felt trapped by comments, mainly from cis women, about how I was supposed to embody womanhood:

- It's unhygienic.
- Don't get a pixie cut, you'll look butch.
- You need to do this because it's the norm.
- People will judge you.
- It's unfortunate.
- We have to go through pain to look beautiful.
- You're expecting acceptance from people too much.
- It's what women need to do.
- You won't get dates.
- You can't show it, it's disgusting.
- Your body hair is dirt.

Oh God, let me be free.

I've denied this possibility for a while. I have privilege that others don't and I don't want to take away space. I'm just trying to get out of societal expectations. It's just internalized misogyny. I don't experience body dysphoria and I don't worry about not finding a gender-neutral bathroom. I'm not enough. But I know now that the experience of gender is infinite, and my feelings count.

The last chapter of Virginia Woolf's *A Room of One's Own* resonates with me so much right now that I'm about to cry happy tears. Her theory doesn't apply to everyone and I don't agree with all of it, but I believe that it does validate my perceptions about myself. Woolf believed that each person had both masculinity and femininity. She posited that in order for a person to fully realize their creative potential and have an expansive view of the world, they must fuse their masculinity and femininity together and be androgynous. If a person views the world through a strictly masculine lens or a strictly feminine lens, then their full self isn't completely realized and their perspective is less open. Her description of androgyny is one of the most beautiful things I've ever read: "...the androgynous mind is resonant and porous; that it transmits emotion without impediment; that it is naturally creative, incandescent and undivided."[70] That sentence captures everything I want to become.

I'm examining why I felt more powerful when I was David Wilde— is it because I've been taught to equate manhood with power? Or is it because I felt my entire self's potential? After thinking about it for a while, I think it's the latter. David Wilde is androgynous and embraces masculinity and femininity. Men who are aligned with femininity and queer identity typically aren't viewed by other people as "powerful." That's because their image of power is embedded in cultural ideas of masculinity. David Wilde's power comes from loving all aspects of his being and shattering gender norms to pieces. David Wilde embodies androgynous power. As him, I defy all of the gender binary's rules, and I transcend the boundaries that society wishes to place on me. It is power in rejecting a system that perpetuates toxic masculinity, misogyny, and cis-heteronormativity. Through creating him, I inadvertently brought to life a side of me that I never knew existed. I need to explore that. I can't deny my lack of connection to the gender binary any longer, and I don't think I'd be fully happy if I lived according to societal expectations of gender. I wish to integrate Eryn Star and David Wilde into one empowered being, onstage and offstage. I imagine myself being gentler, more self-confident, more charismatic, more present. When I'm offstage, I feel trapped because I'm not allowed to fully embody androgynous power; I'm restricted to strict womanhood/femininity and that isn't how I want to live my life. I don't want to be restricted to strict manhood/masculinity either. I'm still searching for language sometimes. I'll always need more language and I'll always be asking myself questions. This is what I should be doing; questioning and taking time is essential. Shifts in my thoughts over time are natural and okay. What I do know is that examining my gender identity and gender expression will help unlock my potential as a human being.

I am becoming.

---

*Eryn is an autistic androgyne pan Jewish humanist person who is passionate about disability and queer justice. They love sci-fi shows, Shakespeare, and Sufjan Stevens.*

# The Girlhood That Wasn't Mine (The Spaces I Cannot Enter)

Kit Mead (they/them/their)

I do not remember how old I was when I knew I was not like the other girls. I do not remember how old I was when I was told, indirectly, that saying "not like other girls" is "internalized misogyny" from people on the internet. I do not remember how I responded. I remember how old I was when I was diagnosed as autistic, shortly before high school. I remember how old I was when I finally discovered I was non-binary, in late college.

Even before then, I identified as LGBTQ (I found the word queer later, in college), shifting identities around, trying to fit them like Jenga tiles. I worried if I chose the wrong one the wrath of both community members and outsiders alike would tumble down on me. Nowadays, it's mostly, "Hell if I know specifically, but queer, definitely that."

Trying to peg specific LGBTQ+ identities on me gets very long in the label department, and then I start getting a bit confused about what exact, specific terminology to use, and then I start wondering if I'm really actually this or that, and *what if I am a faker*?

(I've even worried that out loud, "What if I'm not autistic?" at a leadership program for autistic college students, which was met with a chuckle and a, "You are definitely autistic, Kit.") Being autistic definitely has something to do with the "What am I?" debacle that goes on in my brain at times, or that book I could write entitled "Alexithymia: That feeling when...uh, what is that feeling?"

That doesn't make me less queer or non-binary, especially because, in addition, I have severe generalized anxiety and complex post-traumatic stress disorder, and that makes my memory spotty about my feelings through time. Also, can we not tell people they have to be one fixed identity their entire life and that they were wrong, necessarily, if they realize they are not an identity later? It's up to an individual person to decide if they were truly wrong and never that identity or if something inside them just changed.

I am 26 years old now. Five years down the road, I've bounced around a bit trying to "make sure." I still land on non-binary. I just am *not a woman*. (Even if sometimes I think non-binary is just a word I use because nothing else adequately covers my gender feels. Much like queer covers a lot of stuff.) That's okay. It would be okay even if I realized maybe I was a woman, or that my experiences were, at best, not satisfied by either "non-binary" or "woman."

I am at best an outsider in queer spaces. I have written about this. These spaces tend to be loud. They do not tend to consider autistic and neurodivergent access needs, often not physical ones either. I am afraid of saying anything about the noise, the brightness, the lack of social accommodation for fear of silencing those around me. I do not want to silence people's pride. I just want to be included in that.

But I live, I laugh, I mourn separately. We are often siloed. Autistic people are often LGBTQ+. Vice versa: LGBTQ+ people are often autistic. Mental health disabilities run high in my communities. Suicide. And if not that, there is discrimination, murder, filicide, violence.

But I don't take part in queer spaces often anymore, if at all. My mobility is limited by Ehlers-Danlos syndrome/pain flares, severe stress, money issues, mental health flares, and easy sensory overload. I spend most of my time online, in explicitly autism-friendly spaces, or in the coffee shop about 50 yards from my residence. I don't feel part of the queer, non-binary narrative. I never really have, when I can't be in the spaces meant for us from about nine kinds of inaccessibility at any given moment.

I feel fortunate that I have found autistic spaces that are often queer-centered, competent on non-binary issues, and the like. I know it is not so for some people. The narrative is predominantly of white, cisgender, straight men. Many people do not get their identities centered, even in the spaces I frequent, and I hope we can do better.

But I also hope queer spaces do better.

So, well before I was 14 and diagnosed with autism, I was "not like the other girls," because it wasn't even that my movement, my communication, my sensory experience were different, *I just wasn't a girl*. I did not know enough to know that non-binary was a word I could use to describe my experience.

Well before I was 21, finding out I was non-binary, I was "not like the other girls," because I was autistic, and *not a girl*. I was not a girl, but before I knew that, I was still not like the other girls. That is not just internalized misogyny. While it can be a function of the patriarchy that tells girls they should hate each other, telling everyone that this is the only possible explanation is also a function of ableism, anti-LGBTQ+ stances, and various other -isms.

I am queer and non-binary regardless of the spaces I can enter. I am autistic and have multiple disabilities, regardless of the spaces I can enter. I am queer and non-binary and autistic regardless of my imperfect place in all the narratives. I am all of these things at once. A common adage on Tumblr is "getting into a box of your own accord is quite different than someone putting you in the box, as any cat will tell you." No one can take my labels—*my identities and experiences*—from me.

---

*Kit Mead is a queer/non-binary multiply-disabled advocate, writer, and conversion student to Judaism. They are frequently found with their cat, writing, drawing, or in coffee shops.*

# Finding Myself: In Parallel

*Andren Copass (he/him/his or they/them/their)*

I didn't know I was different.

Not at first, anyway.

I thought I was normal. I thought I was like everyone else. Or more accurately, that everyone was like me. I thought it was normal to want to line up your toys. I thought everyone born female would dread the day their breasts grew in. I couldn't understand how other people could possibly deal with the horrible sensation of things lightly touching their skin. Surely everyone would prefer to be a guy, if they had the choice.

Eventually I did start to realize that not everyone was like me. Apparently, most women actually liked being women! They looked forward to growing breasts, and enjoyed them when they showed up! Who could possibly imagine such a thing! Right alongside these realizations, my mom tried to get me to play with my toys the "right" way instead of lining them up. I didn't understand—lining them up was fun and satisfying; pretending to have a tea party was not at all fun and very weird. As for all the other stuff—the inability to eat mushy food, the confusion over what is and is not sarcasm, the being different—apparently I was just weak. No one else started screaming over schedule changes, over textures, over sensory overload and things just being Too Much. They were temper tantrums, I was being manipulative, if I just would just try harder I could be like a normal person. Why wouldn't I try harder?

I started to hate myself. What was wrong with me? Why couldn't I enjoy my body the way other people did? Why did everything hurt so much all the time? Why couldn't I understand other people? Why was I different?!

I didn't know why. I wouldn't know why until well into adulthood. No matter how hard I tried, I couldn't pray away any of my difficulties. No amount of trying harder made the world any less bright and loud. There was just no way to convince myself to enjoy being a woman—and I tried. I *really* tried. For years, I tried.

It didn't go well.

I utterly loathed the body I had developed. I spent my life alternating between wearing huge, shapeless clothing to try to hide it and trying to embrace the gender people were insisting I had to be. I also loathed myself. My weakness. All the many ways that I could not understand people, the things I could not cope with, and I didn't understand any of it. I didn't even hear the word "Asperger's" or "autistic" until I was 18. But the time I learned that some people are trans, I had resigned myself to being a woman. That's all there was for me.

Things stayed that way for a long time, around ten years, in fact. That is entirely too long. No one should have to wait that long.

And yet, things did eventually change. With supportive friends, being fortunate in the resources I had at my disposal, and definitely some scrambling around in the mental health world, I more fully learned who I was. In those ten years between first hearing the word "Asperger's" and finally being diagnosed, I learned more and more about it. Gradually, more and more people were bringing it up to me on their own. By my late 20s I, and everyone around me, was pretty sure I was on the autism spectrum—and knowing *why* things were so hard all the time was such a huge relief. Suddenly all these things that people had judged me for my whole life fitted into a known pattern. Suddenly I had resources to help me understand what was hurting me and why.

As for being trans, that was mostly about just accepting that the way other people experience gender and the way I experience gender are, in fact, very different. First I bought a binder. Then I started trying on different pronouns—how did "he" feel on me, anyway? Turns out, it felt good. I started to wear clothes that just felt good for me to wear, regardless of perceived masculinity or femininity. I learned what I like to wear, rather than simply what I don't like to wear.

Also, I got top surgery. That was a pretty big deal too. Suddenly my body fits me, in a way it hadn't in so long.

So here I am. I'm in my late 30s and I am finally coming into my own. I am autistic. I am transmasculine. I am good enough. I am strong.

---

*Andren is a confused kitty-cat from Claymont. He likes to play with other kitties, make things, and cuddle, and occasionally manages to write something.*

# Steps to an Identity

*Rae Kersley (they/them/their)*

**1.**
ask for makeup
because it's pretty and girly and fun,
and the social scripts you can't yet name
say it's what you should want,
and it's a mask a disguise
a layer of performativity between you and the world.

ask for make-up
you have no idea how to apply.

**2.**
stop asking for makeup
because you're not going to spend time,
every day,
putting something on your face
when all the best
brightest things you can do with it

you have to take off
before you go outside.

**3.**
fail to learn coding
when your mother tries to teach you.

learn binaries anyway:
girl–boy
*pink–blue*
girly girl–tomboy
*pink–red*
weak–strong
*pink–green*

start avoiding pink.

**4.**
fall in love like *relatability*
with the characters
who don't know how to people,
who don't know how to gender—
robots and aliens and monsters and

only realize years later
why.

**5.**
hold yourself tight.
tight
tight
tighter

curl up close to sleep,
dig fingers into flesh and squeeze,
hold yourself tight,
just because you need—
pressure
pressure
pressure

*stimulation*

**6.**

learn how to perform femininity
from female characters
written by men—
*swinging hips*
*swishing skirts*
*sidelong glances*
*red red lips*

learn how to perform masculinity
by default

**7.**

don't bother thinking about your gender

**8.**

find out there are options
(*non-binary*)
find out there are words
(*autistic*)
find yourself

**9.**

think about gender

think about identity

think and think and think
your new favorite song
playing on loop
ad infinitum

**10.**

pick a label
pick another

pick and pick and pick—

look for something to encompass all of you
*exactly*
accuracy and precision and—

*"does your red look like mine?"*
examine external descriptions
of internal experiences, and—

*"does your non-binary feel like mine?"*
take words with nebulous meanings,
apply to lives with nebulous identities—

look for accurate precision
(keep looking)

**11.**
start wearing makeup again,
blues and greens and glitter everywhere.
start wearing pink again,
sequins and shoes and bowties.
cut your hair and grow your hair and
do both at once.

try to make the outside match
the inside you can barely articulate.

**12.**
wear a binder for the first time and
bounce
bounce
*bounce*
for joy
over how flat you look,
and over

pressure
pressure
pressure
*stimulation*

wear a corset for the first time and
spin
spin
*spin*
with glee
over your new costume
and over

pressure
pressure
pressure
*stimulation*

**13.**
learn how to perform yourself—
*go perform*

---

*Rae is a queer autistic creator from Australia. They play the harp and viola and write all sorts of things—mostly queer spec-fic and poetry.*

# So Typical, Yet So Atypical

*Kerry Chin (he/him/his)*

My name is Kerry. I'm an autistic trans man. I'm also aromantic and asexual. That probably makes me sound like a stereotypical Tumblr user.

On being stereotypical, I'm also an electrical engineer. I work in the rail industry, and I'm particularly appreciated for my computer skills at work. It's the perfect career for an autistic person.

Jokes aside, as much as I fit into a lot of stereotypes, I would also say that my experience isn't typical among the autistic and/or transgender people I know.

## EARLY DIAGNOSIS

Despite being assigned female at birth, I received a formal diagnosis of Asperger's syndrome at age seven. At the time, I was living in Hong Kong and studying at a local primary school. As far as I know, understanding of autism and other developmental differences was not widespread at the time. As such, even receiving a diagnosis at all was exceptional.

As an adult, I learned that autistic women were often not identified as being autistic until their teenage years or even later. According to some autistic women I've met, in the 1990s (when I was a child), the dominant view among medical professionals was that autism simply didn't exist in girls and women.

Ironically, as much as I am aware of the fact that women are less likely to be correctly identified as being autistic (and therefore less likely to have access to the appropriate support), as an adult, I have met plenty of men whose behavior reminds me exactly of myself as a child, and thus I feel that perhaps if I were assigned male at birth, my mother might not have perceived my autistic behavior as an issue that required professional assessment, and I would not have received my diagnosis so early.

I have heard various explanations for why girls are less likely to be diagnosed as autistic than boys, including that girls are better at imitating their peers' behavior, and that their "special interests" are often seen as typical interests for girls. I do not identify with either of those descriptions.

## SCHOOL

Even though I was fortunate enough to have known about being autistic early on, I did not truly accept myself as such until much later. Even though it was my mother who took me to a child psychologist for an assessment, both of my parents also tried their best to pretend that the diagnosis was incorrect.

In my primary school years, most of my classmates did not like me, and I did not understand why, but I was not interested in befriending them anyway. I had good grades at school and was known for being "smart," but a lot of my classmates also called me a "retard." Some of them would even say the two things in the same conversation without noticing the contradiction in the meanings of those words.

In my later years of primary school, after I had received my formal diagnosis, my parents decided to send me to an international school, and they even paid for me to receive "additional support." In primary school, this included working with a school counselor who gave me a lot of advice about making friends. I do not remember the details. In my secondary school years, it meant getting support from a teacher's aide in some classes, although the teacher's aide was primarily there to support the students with intellectual disabilities. In a lot of situations, this "support" was actually counterproductive in the sense that I did not need any help with my studies, and having someone there to nag me only increased my frustration as well as wasted my time. I also did not appreciate being grouped in with the students with intellectual disabilities. However, in the long term, this did at least help me develop patience, as I often had to help them with class work.

At some point, my parents received a letter from the school saying that I had made progress in my development and now fell into a category of needing less support than I previously did. I remember my mother taking the opportunity to tell me that I probably never really had Asperger's syndrome anyway.

Even though I grew up living with both of my parents, my father has always spoken of autism as if he was never aware of my original diagnosis. I've taken this to mean that he is intentionally ignoring that aspect of my life, as he has always remembered other details about me such as my dietary preferences and interests, often even more than my mother has.

In terms of my gender identity, I was also one of those people who "always knew." I didn't know of the word "transgender" until much later, but I always knew that I was "really a boy." Throughout my childhood, I had always resented being told that I was a girl, but I also knew I would get in trouble if I tried to explain to the adults in my life that I was really a boy.

I consider myself lucky that my parents were not extreme in enforcing gender roles, in the sense that I was never specifically stopped from doing things "because I was a girl." I had always been allowed to play with toys that were stereotypically "for boys," and my mother did not particularly pressure me into wearing skirts and dresses. I did have to wear skirts and dresses as part of my school uniform, but that was the least of my issues with school.

## THE INTERNET

I joke that I'm a stereotypical Tumblr user, but in many ways, I'm most definitely not. I'm athletic, and I spend most of my waking hours outside home at various social events. I've never watched any shows on Netflix before, and I can't imagine having time for that any time soon.

I wasn't always like that. When I was at school, most of my classmates didn't like me, and I wasn't interested in being friends with them either. There were a few classmates who tried to be my friends, but I had nothing in common with them and found them annoying. I was clumsy and not good at any kind of physical activity, so I did not participate in any extracurricular sports. Other than going to school, I spent most of my time at home. As such, I used to spend a lot of time reading, watching television, and playing video games. In my secondary school years, I started using the internet, and I got really into it.

I discovered the concept of feminism some time in my early teens. Having always been told that some of the things I liked were "for boys," the message of gender equality strongly resonated with me. However, it also made me less comfortable with my transgender identity, as I believed that I ought to be proud of defying traditional gender roles.

Making friends on the internet was a very important part of my social development. Most of my internet friends were located overseas, so I did not have the opportunity to meet them in person. However, from having internet friends, I realized that it was worthwhile to make the effort to communicate with people, and that it was possible to find "the right people."

At the time, I never thought to look for information about being transgender (because I didn't know the term), but through an internet friend's blog, I stumbled on the concept of asexuality. At age 14, I considered it logical for some people to be asexual, because if it was possible to be attracted to the same gender, the "opposite" gender, or both, then it made sense that some people were attracted to neither. (I'm now aware that this is an overly simplistic idea of genders and sexual orientations, but I didn't know any better back then.) Still, it did not occur to me that I was asexual, and I believed that I would eventually start experiencing sexual attraction "when I grow up." I remember a classmate asking me if I was a lesbian. I said I wasn't, but she wasn't going to believe me.

At age 15, I moved to Sydney, Australia. In my new school, I often heard my classmates discussing crushes and boyfriends, and I was completely uninterested. Eventually, I concluded that perhaps I was asexual after all. I started reading more about the topic, and somehow, I found links to information about autism through one of the asexuality blogs. I read a bit more into the topic, but it still wasn't a major focus at the time.

## UNIVERSITY

My grades in high school weren't as good as they were when I was in primary school because I wasn't used to putting effort into studying, but I still did well enough to get my first preference in university admission. It was a five-year double degree of electrical engineering and arts.

I enjoyed studying the subjects I chose, and in my first year at university I won an award for "achievement among women engineers."

As much as I was happy about having achieved enough to qualify for an award, I also felt strange about winning an award that was meant for women.

When I started university, I was still a shy person who didn't especially enjoy face-to-face socializing. Still, there were always opportunities to talk to my classmates while waiting for classes to start, and in my first year of university, a lot of my classmates made the effort to introduce themselves to me. I also decided to join some of the clubs and societies. Eventually, I got the hang of socializing and grew to enjoy it.

Among all the people I met at university, there were some gay students who often spent time in the university's Queerspace (an autonomous room on campus open to all queer-identifying and questioning students), and even before I came out to them (either as asexual or transgender), they invited me to join them there. In the Queerspace, I eventually met other transgender people and learned about the various ways people can affirm their gender. At the time, it was fairly common to speak about the gender that one "identifies as," and those conversations were always tricky because I knew very well that I did not identify as female.

Around my third year at university, I eventually decided to try binding and packing. Wearing a packer felt just right. Binding was physically uncomfortable, but it was still more comfortable than wearing a bra. From then onwards, I realized that there was no going back, and that I would have to come out eventually. I had my hair cut short at the front, and apparently, even that was enough for me to occasionally be perceived as male by strangers. I started attending a local transgender support group, and I found that I shared a lot of experiences with the other participants.

From the third year onwards, as I spent more and more time on social activities, my grades declined, and I failed two subjects in one semester. Still, I went on to complete my degree within the prescribed five years of full-time study, which apparently puts me in the minority among people I know.

## BICYCLES

On receiving my first timetable at university, I realized that I was going to need a bicycle because I had back-to-back classes on opposite ends of the campus. Luckily, I already had one. I used to ride it in the park at weekends, and it had been gathering dust in the garage during my final year of high school. Little did I know at the time that choosing to ride a bicycle for transport was going to be a major turning point in my life.

I started out bringing my bicycle to campus by train just to ride between my classes. The train station was only 1 km away from the campus, and that was enough exercise for a day back then. However, I got used to it quickly, and by the end of the first semester, I was riding all the way to campus and back home regularly (10 km each way).

I don't think I have an anxiety disorder, nor have I ever received a formal diagnosis for one, but I had been a highly anxious person from my teens onwards. (The distinction is important: almost everyone feels anxious at some point in life, but that is not the same as having an anxiety disorder.) I discovered that the physical exertion of riding my bicycle helped me achieve temporary calmness, and that helped me socialize comfortably. In those years, I was highly dependent on my bicycle.

Even though I made a lot of friends at university, other bicycle riders were conspicuously missing from my social life. By chance, towards the end of my first year at university, I found out about a cycling event through an emailing list. I showed up and met other cyclists, who invited me to other cycling events. Within a year or so, I had become one of the most well-known cyclists in Sydney.

The majority of people I met through cycling groups were middle-aged men. I got along very well with them, which is perhaps unsurprising, as it is common for autistic people to prefer the company of people who are not their own age. Unfortunately, some of these men showed sexual and romantic interest in me eventually. As much as this was an inconvenience, I continued to spend time with these men because I enjoyed their company, even if it meant spending a lot of time rejecting their advances. In retrospect, I realize that most women would have recognized such situations as dangerous and avoided these men.

In my university years, before I accepted myself as transgender, I wasn't a "tomboy" in terms of my clothing style. At some point, I was introduced to the concept of "cycle chic," and I was inspired to wear skirts and dresses more often. I also enjoyed wearing high heels, which were good for gripping bicycle pedals. Also, like many autistic people, I had a habit of toe-walking, and the high heels made it look more natural.

When I eventually started binding, I rode my bicycle with the binder on, which I would not recommend to anyone else. My suitors noticed the absence of my breasts and were disappointed. They asked me to stop binding, but I did not consider their opinions at all. I eventually shocked one of my suitors by showing him my packer. He was convinced that I was only doing this to upset him, but he gave up soon after anyway.

I eventually met a more supportive friend through other bicycle events. Not long after we met, we started having regular in-depth conversations via email, and I soon told him about being autistic and transgender. One time, he did not reply to my email for a few days, and when he eventually wrote back, he apologized for his brief response and explained that he needed solitude. At that point in my life, I had grown to distance myself from the childhood memories where I had the more overtly autistic behaviors, and I would wince whenever anyone described autistic traits. The entire conversation was a painful reminder of my childhood memories, and I cried my eyes out. Still, I was not upset at my friend. I appreciated the affirmation of the need for solitude, and with his words, I had the opportunity to reconcile with the memories of who I was as a child with the person I grew up to be.

## WORK EXPERIENCE

Work experience was one of the requirements for the engineering degree. By my third year, I began to look for internships. At the time, I knew very little about job applications, and was not able to find a job in time. My uncle ended up getting me a summer job through his connections, so I went back to Hong Kong during my summer holiday and started working at my first job.

Since this was on a construction site, I was told to buy my own steel-capped safety shoes, and on the first day, I was provided with the rest of the standard personal protective equipment, including a high-vis vest, a hard hat, safety glasses, and a pair of earplugs. As one does, I tried those items on when I received them. It was a life-changing moment as I discovered that the earplugs blocked out background noise and allowed me to understand speech more easily. I also really liked my steel-capped boots, as the weight made me feel more relaxed, and also helped me balance better.

Socially, I did not fit in at all in this blue-collar workplace in Hong Kong. Everything about me stood out, from my gait to my lack of eye contact with other people. I had been away from Hong Kong for long enough that I might as well be a foreigner, but at the same time, I did not physically look foreign. In contrast, I believe that a lot of people in Sydney attributed my autistic behaviors to cultural differences. For example, in one of my linguistics classes, I learned that in Chinese culture, it is respectful to look away instead of making eye contact as Anglo-Australians would. I would never have known this from living in Hong Kong, which had a British-influenced culture due to its colonial history. Still, it is convenient for me that other people assume this to be true, as I then "get away" with not making eye contact.

The summer at my overseas job went by quickly, and I went back to Sydney for my final year at university. In my final year of university, I applied to a few graduate programs. My mother had never objected to me having short hair before, but when I was called for a job interview, she was suddenly worried about my hairstyle. Her worries turned out to be unfounded. I passed the interview, and while the process took a few months, I received a job offer about a month before my final exams.

## GRADUATE PROGRAM

I waited until I finished my studies to begin my medical transition, because I anticipated that my parents might not accept me, and I wanted to be prepared for the worst-case scenario where they kicked me out of their home.

First, I needed a psychiatrist's approval to start taking hormones. In the first appointment, the psychiatrist asked, "Have you heard of autism spectrum disorders?", which I found somewhat discouraging. He also gave me a flyer about coping with anxiety even though it wasn't why I was there. I remember it to have generic information such as taking deep breaths, which I never found helpful.

I think being autistic put me at a disadvantage in terms of getting the approval for hormones, but I got it eventually after a few more sessions. Starting on testosterone made me calm down considerably, beyond what I could achieve just by exercising, and it happened within a day of my first injection. To me, just this one effect alone was worth all the effort.

By then, I was in the second of my four six-month rotations in my graduate program. In my male-dominated workplace, it was common for my colleagues to address groups as "gentlemen." As such, when I encountered people I did not already know, I was often unsure whether they perceived me as male, or simply did not notice my presence in the group.

My third rotation was a significant stage in my transition. By then, a lot of the physical changes that I expected from testosterone had taken place, and I looked sufficiently masculine that most strangers perceived me as male. I had stopped binding my chest as it was too uncomfortable and no longer worth it now that I looked masculine enough. Work had been particularly awkward, as my colleagues initially perceived me as a man but later assumed that they were incorrect when someone who knew me from before referred to me with she/her pronouns. Even then, overall it wasn't too bad as I got along particularly well with my supervisor because he told me early on that sometimes he did not make eye contact with people during conversations. That was good news to me, and I told him that I was autistic and therefore had the same problem. I eventually told him that I was transgender too. By the end of this rotation, he said he had learned a lot about what it meant to be autistic and transgender from me.

For my fourth rotation, I worked in an office building with really harsh fluorescent lights, and I quickly became unwell due to my sensory issues. I was feeling tired and dizzy, and couldn't concentrate on anything. I couldn't even play video games at home. I asked my placement manager if it was acceptable to remove the fluorescent tube directly above my desk, and to my surprise, he agreed to it. He contacted the human resources (HR) department to ask why they did not inform him about my needs ahead of time, and in that process, he discovered that I was on record as being female. He was not impressed that I had been withholding information from the HR department, and told me to arrange a meeting with a diversity officer to discuss my support needs.

Even though the official stance of the company was to support diversity and non-discrimination, I had been hesitant to be officially on record as having a disability because I believed that individual colleagues might still discriminate against me. The diversity officer told me that I seemed very "high-functioning," and my record indicated that my work performance had been more than satisfactory thus far. She also told me about the company's special traineeship program for people with disabilities. As much as I understood that she was making a serious effort at her job, I did not actually find any of this reassuring. Still, knowing that the company now had my details on record was a relief, as it was officially not a secret.

Removing the fluorescent light above my desk made the office environment more comfortable, but by then I was already very unwell, and I wasn't getting any better. My mother noticed that I looked tired, and after I told her that my workplace had already been allowing adjustments, she asked if there was anything else I needed to make me feel better. I decided to look for tinted glasses to reduce the glare. The ones I chose were marketed at people with migraines, but they turned out to be suitable for my needs. After starting to use them at work, I felt better almost immediately, but it took almost an entire year before I was completely well again. In this time, I grew more comfortable with accepting myself for who I was, and I believe that the support at work was an important cue for my mother to follow.

## FROM GRADUATE TO PROFESSIONAL

Even though the graduate program was only supposed to last for two years, I stayed on for over three years before I finally found a permanent role in the organization. I went into an operational role with important responsibilities and absolute deadlines. Contrary to what one might expect for people who are naturally anxious, I enjoyed the high-pressure environment from day one, and I gradually became calmer as I adapted to the stress of my job. I also became more comfortable with talking on the telephone, which I had previously disliked for most of my life.

As much as I excelled in the technical side of my job, the communication side was a steep learning curve. My job involved declining people's requests when they did not meet the guidelines, and it took me a while to learn to politely say "no" without causing offence. I soon learned to eliminate the possibility of sounding rude by using highly standardized templates. I was lucky that my manager put in the effort to clearly explain what exactly it was that I did wrong, so that I had a fair chance at not making the same mistakes. He and I had our own misunderstandings early on. He asked if I felt the increase in responsibility as I went from the graduate program to this important role. I said "no" because I believed that responsibility was a given no matter what one's role is, and saying "yes" meant that one was an irresponsible person, whereas he took the "no" to be a lack of appreciation for the seriousness of the role. As he got to know me better over time, my perspective made more sense to him.

By this point in time, people meeting me for the first time consistently perceived me as male. Even though I still occasionally encountered people who had met me before I started on testosterone, most of them either did not remember previously meeting me or knew what was going on and correctly referred to me with he/him pronouns in the third person without requiring any explanation. I had only heard two people stumble over my pronouns, and these were people I rarely needed to contact.

Over the years, I have tried the various formulations of testosterone. I started with Sustanon, but that was a fortnightly injection and it was a major inconvenience to go to the clinic to get it (I was scared to self-inject). I later changed to Reandron. That was one injection every 12 weeks, which had the advantage of being relatively infrequent as well as lining up with paperwork lead times at work so that it was easy for me to track. However, I experienced symptoms of low hormone levels towards the end of each injection cycle, and with my demanding job, I simply could not afford to lose one week in every 12, so I changed to Testogel, which I applied daily in the morning.

During the graduate program, I was reluctant to take leave for extended periods as I did not want to miss too much of each rotation. Consequently, I had a lot of leave saved up by the time I got a permanent role. Still, it was another year before I finally had top surgery. Even though I had been on testosterone for four years by then, I had not told my parents about my medical transition, so I strategically scheduled the surgery for a date when they were overseas. A friend drove me home from hospital, and visited daily to help me brush my hair and get dressed until I could move my arms normally again.

Just over a year later, my GP recommended that I get a hysterectomy, as by then I had been on testosterone for almost six years. I liked the idea of not having a uterus, but I also wasn't particularly in a hurry to go for the surgery. Still, I went ahead with it, and it resulted in surprising improvements to my quality of life. While I became a lot less nervous after starting on testosterone, the hysterectomy brought me to a whole new level of calmness that I had never experienced before. At the same time, my overall energy levels also increased drastically after the surgery. As with every other part of my transition, I only wish I had done this earlier.

## MY PARENTS

My parents first found out I was transgender during the first year of my transition, and they did not approve at the time. I went ahead with the transition anyway. Conveniently, since I normally spent a lot of time outside the home, they could not monitor what exactly I was doing.

Still, eventually, my mother noticed a Testogel sachet when she was emptying the rubbish bin. I had been on testosterone for five years by then, and its effect on my well-being was clear. My mother was relieved that it was prescribed by a doctor and not something I had randomly bought from the internet. Last year, I went swimming with her for the first time after my chest surgery. It had been just over two years, and my scars were still very clear, but she said my body looked good anyway.

When my mother first found out I was transgender, she said she had always wanted a son. It was the ultimate testament to the expression "be careful what you wish for."

My father has mostly refrained from asking questions about my body, perhaps because it would be awkward for a father to talk about his "daughter's" body. He did make one comment about me getting muscular not long after I started on testosterone, but that was easily attributed to my athletic lifestyle. I've taken his silence to mean that, as with my autism, he simply did not want to face the truth. I do not plan to bring up the discussion any time soon with him.

## WHERE TO NEXT?

That's my life so far. I'm living proof that one can be autistic, transgender, and be happy against all odds. Even though I am comfortable with these aspects of myself, I continue to spend time in groups for autistic and transgender people, because there is no substitution for spending time with people who are "just like me." That's not due to a lack of socializing opportunities. I spend so much time socializing that I'm hardly ever at home. I sing in a choir, go running regularly with a group, run a Scrabble club, and build Mardi Gras floats. I still work at the same company that I joined right after graduating from university, and at the time of writing, I have been there for just over seven years. I suppose that's now the one thing that makes me atypical more than anything else.

---

*Kerry is an autistic trans man who has a habit of taking on too many responsibilities. He rides the most conspicuous bicycle in Sydney.*

# A Plea of Things I Would Like You to Know

*Shannon Shannon (Shannon/Shannon/Shannon's)*

Among the abundance of life's treasures and treacherous reasons for me to be stressed, I have been graced with the added joy of worry and misinterpretation. While I am granted relief from some exhaustion due to privilege and circumstance, I continue to find life confusing. To help create a world in which I, and others, might be welcomed/might be accepted/might be loved/might be listened to, here are some things I would like you to know. To further disorient you, like I so often am, I have included some things I have experienced in the long process of seeking a diagnosis.

What's the connection between friend and enemy and always and never and apple and grapes and create this shape from three of these six shapes and memorize these groups of words on the computer and form this pattern from these blocks and what were those words on the computer and answer these math word problems and memorize these numbers and say them backwards and what were those words again from the computer and answer these random questions and memorize this new list of words spoken to you and here's another list of words and tell me the first list of words and tell me what these pictures are showing.

Sometimes when you ask me about my gender and expect me to respond, I can't figure out what you want. Sometimes I think my explanations of gender serve more of a purpose to you than me. I don't need these words to understand who I am, yet you require them from me.

List all of the words that start with "A" and all of the words that start with "S" and all of the "boy" names and all of the animals and what were the words from the first list that were furniture and what do these words mean and hit the spacebar when a letter appears *but not* "X" and how many numbers did I just say and how many letters and hit the spacebar when a low sound is followed by a high sound and read out the colors of the shapes in order and read the names of the colors and read the names of the colors but not the color the word is in and read the word if it's in a box but read the color of the word if not in a box.

In order to access help and understanding I am required, in all aspects, to fit a certain code. I must be upset with my body. I must want physical change. I must choose from the limited list of socially acceptable pronouns. I must yearn to be masculine. I must have a desired end goal of transformation. I must have special interests and those interests must align with what is assumed of me by gender. I must be extraordinary at something since I am not considered to be less than at other things. I must be socially unaware. I must be frightened.

I must be helpless.

I must be helpless.

I must be helpless.

Stare at these six shapes for ten seconds and draw them and look at them again and draw and one more time and draw this other very detailed shape and put the pegs in the holes with your right hand and now with your left and tap this thing with your palm down with just your pointer finger on your right hand and now your left and now your right and now your left and now your right and now your left and now your right and right again and again and again and draw those six shapes from memory and tell me if these shapes were in that group of six shapes and figure out the pattern of different colors/numbers/shapes.

I believe I am many things and I do not require a diagnosis code on a piece of paper I paid too much for to tell me that. I am allowed to be content with my body. I am allowed to love it, even though I often do not. I am allowed to want change and I am allowed to include changing my mind in that. I am allowed to not use pronouns. I am allowed to use all pronouns. I am allowed to not care until I do and you are not required to understand why. I am allowed to love dresses and I am allowed to be annoyed when you assume I should feel concerned about that. I am allowed a static transformation, a rapid transformation, an inner transformation. (Since what are we, but bodies always shifting and molding at our own individual pace?) I am allowed to have special interests within and beyond those previously studied and understood. I am allowed to not know anything about science and also know everything about reality television and pop culture. I am allowed to consider those things to be interests, even if you do not. I am allowed to be just okay. I am allowed to be beyond and below the assumed norm. I am allowed to have friends. I am allowed to be uncomfortable with that sometimes. I am allowed to live, allowed to thrive, and still allowed to seek help from myself and others.

As hard as I try to be understood, as non-binary, as autistic, I deserve to have you try too. So let me ask you:

What's the connection between transgender and autism?

I'll give you time to think. I won't take notes. I'd just like to know.

---

*Shannon's many identities are constantly changing, but consistently very tired. Shannon loves reading and making art in cozy coffee shops and everything about Shannon's dog.*

# One Step at a Time

Lee N *(they/them/their)*

Denial, anger, bargaining, depression, and acceptance. These are the five stages of grief. None of us is immune to grief, and everyone who has experienced this emotion knows of its transformative power to change a person. For most people, the grieving process comes in two parts. Part 1, the loss. The loss could be of a friendship, home, or even a community. In my case, I lost all three. However, the process does not end with that aching despair of loss. Part 2 is picking up the pieces after what happened and beginning anew. This is the part that I am currently at in my life. After losing my apartment, my best friend, and my support group all at once, I have had to rebuild my life and grapple with the circumstances that drove me and my best friend apart.

My name is Lee, and I am a queer, non-binary, autistic adult. Although I am proud of these identities now, for a long time I felt as if I was destined to be misunderstood. Growing up, I knew I was very different from other kids, who would frequently bully me for being "weird" and "antisocial." At the time, it didn't make sense to me why it was so hard to connect with people, as if we spoke a different language. I carried this isolation with me like an invisible backpack that seemed to repel people from getting to know me very well.

Therapists and doctors were quick to diagnose me with depression and anxiety, which seemed to satisfy some explanations of my behavior, but I still felt as if something was missing. In fact, I had suspected I was autistic as early as 16, but that was quickly dismissed by a therapist who told me that I couldn't possibly be autistic since their one and only autistic patient did not present their symptoms in the same way I did. I believed her, too. It was ten years later when, ironically, another therapist had me officially tested and confirmed the suspected diagnosis.

In my early 20s, I underwent another personal discovery that was dismissed by others—specifically, the realization that I was non-binary. I remember when I was on a study abroad trip at 21, and I had the brilliant idea to write my preferred name on my Spanish test, sparking my first experience with gender euphoria. Unfortunately, the teacher who collected the test asked me if I was sure this was my name, as if I couldn't remember and only this teacher knew for sure. I told her it was just a nickname. With that reply, I attempted to bury that name, along with my gender identity, for a long time. Nevertheless, once college ended, I was no longer required to answer to my given name. That "nickname" I loved felt more right than my given name. I felt as if I was growing into my body and my gender identity along with it.

There was still a problem, though. True, I was beginning to feel more secure in my identity as a non-binary, neurodivergent person, but I lacked a support system that could even begin to understand what all this meant. My family wasn't an option, and I didn't have many friends. Meanwhile, my peers were getting started on their careers, getting into serious relationships, and moving on, while I was stuck in a rut of confusion and loneliness. Ultimately, I was looking for a community of people who shared similar identities as I did, where I could make a few friends and boost my low self-esteem. Then, at 22, I discovered NeuroQueer.

NeuroQueer (NQ) was a group for people who identified as LGBTQ and neurodivergent. At the time, the meetings were mostly discussion-based meet-up groups where people could share their stories in a safe, supportive environment. Admittedly, things were a little rocky at first. I realized quickly after I joined that NQ was struggling to attract members and find its own identity. Mainly, it lacked structure and connection to the larger LGBTQ and disability communities. Even though there were over 100 members, very few of them would come to meetings since NQ was relatively unknown. This struggle to organize and maintain the group took its toll on the original organizer of NQ who lacked the spoons to continue their role. This necessitated a new organizer to take the reins. So, Ruby, the most enthusiastic member of NQ, took on the challenge.

Ruby was a queer, bipolar woman with post-traumatic stress disorder and my best friend in the group. She worked as a teacher for a grade school in the city. She and I bonded over our shared love of the group, as well as our LGBTQ identities. She was actually the first person I came out to as non-binary. She had a big heart and a true desire to help everyone in the group, and it showed. As she took over, things started to change for the better. More people were joining, meet-ups seemed more structured and organized, and people were having more fun.

I started to get more involved as well, helping Ruby here and there with planning meet-up ideas and events. Eventually I became co-organizer alongside her, and that's when the meet-up group shot to new heights. Working together, she and I collaborated with local LGBTQ and disability-allied groups, expanded our membership, and started planning more exciting meet-ups. We even organized a retreat that was attended by 20 people, which at the time was the largest group to come to a single meet-up. At that retreat, Ruby publicly thanked me for all my hard work with the meet-up and she called me her best friend. I was elated.

Things were going well for such a long time. I loved organizing the group alongside Ruby. It gave me something to focus on, to look forward to, and to pour my heart into. I felt so connected to this group, this one place in my life where I could be myself, and where there was no need to pretend to be cis or neurotypical in order to receive the support I desperately needed. They were a community, a refuge, an oasis where I could be myself. For the first time, it felt as if that backpack of isolation was lifted, and I knew that I would be okay as long as I was a member there.

It was in this space that I first felt a strong sense of access intimacy that was missing from my life. By "access intimacy," I'm referring to the term coined by Korean-American disability activist Mia Mingus, wherein a disabled person's access needs are immediately understood and wholeheartedly met by another person, or in my case, a group of people. It's the feeling of comfort and relaxation I experienced among fellow NQ members who I was able to turn to for help and support in my daily life, without having to justify my identity or existence. In that space, we could count on each other to respect our differing needs and empathize with each other in our shared, lived experiences.

Ruby and I grew closer as well. She even asked me to move in with her, which was exciting for me since I was 26 and still living with my parents. Her apartment was in the city where NQ met each month, so getting to meet-ups was easier than ever. And we had a lot of fun together too. We would go out to eat, watch TV, play games, and shop together for groceries. I would cook for both of us, so that when she got home from work she would have a hot meal waiting for her. We would also tell each other secrets and talk for hours in the evening about everything and nothing. I truly thought the situation couldn't get any better.

However, this didn't last very long. A few months went by, and I underwent a traumatic event. I won't go into the details of what happened, but I was admitted to the ER for psychiatric reasons. At the same time, I noticed Ruby unraveling. She lost her job as a teacher, and she disclosed to me that she wasn't seeing a doctor at the time to prescribe her any medication for her bipolar disorder. It all happened so fast. One evening, I told her about what I was going through, and disclosed to her that I felt a meltdown coming on. She told me she was undergoing some stress as well from being laid off and that she needed a change. Her plan was to move out the apartment as soon as possible, and since I was not on the lease, I was told I had to find somewhere else to live. She gave me a week to leave.

Because Ruby was pressuring me to leave the apartment in such a short amount of time, I had to get a lawyer involved so I was made aware of my rights. My lawyer confirmed that I had 30 days to leave, but Ruby started to escalate the dispute in order to force me out of the apartment sooner. She began by emailing me a list of "rules" for co-existing with her that prohibited me from sitting on her furniture, using her appliances, and even speaking to her. That same day, Ruby called the police on me as a measure to get me to leave the apartment. When that didn't work, she and her mother, a woman who also has mental health issues, ransacked my room and took the bed that I was sleeping on. She started to intentionally misgender me as well, and her cousins also began to partake in the harassment. The situation was becoming unsafe. Finally, as her last act of retaliation against me, Ruby officially banned me from NQ.

The best way I can describe how I felt in that moment was as if someone had pulled out the rug from underneath me. I didn't believe what was happening. We were friends, right? We should have been able to sort things out. I told her that I would get better and that I would do anything to stay, but Ruby was unwilling to compromise. That's when I started to get angry. Not only was I upset about having to move out from this place I called home, I was deeply concerned about the future of my and Ruby's friendship as well as the future of my membership in NQ. Was there any way we resolve this amicably? What should I do? Was it all over? I had so many thoughts swirling in my head, and in trying to process them, I had seemingly initiated the grieving process.

I was angry about what happened for a long time. I couldn't

imagine a future where I could forgive her for what had happened. But as I look back on these events and try to make some sense out of them, I have found a plausible explanation for why things unfolded the way they did. Specifically, in disability discourse, there is a concept called competing access needs. Competing access needs is the idea that some people, in order to be able to participate in a community, need one thing, and other people need a conflicting thing. The key to resolving this issue is not figuring out which need is most real, but acknowledging that we can't accommodate all needs. Although every space should be accessible to every person, even that ideal can still exclude some people.

In the case of me and Ruby, we both had extenuating circumstances that ended up making us incompatible. Specifically, Ruby was undergoing a stressful life event, exacerbated by being bipolar without medication; I was going through trauma-induced mental distress. Both circumstances are valid, but we couldn't accommodate them both while living together. We ended up triggering each other. NQ was never going to be a space where both of us could co-exist given what we were both going through. The harsh reality in this case was that we were both going through difficulties at the same time, and neither of us had the spoons to deal with our own and each other's needs.

Almost a year has gone by since I have had any contact with NQ or Ruby. Eventually the anger subsided, but the depression I felt after losing so much at once was almost unbearable. There was a hole in my heart where the support of my friend and community used to be. I basically had to move back in with my parents and try to go on without them. This has proven to be extremely difficult, but not impossible. I still had some supports, and these proved to be crucial in moving me from depression to acceptance. I had my therapist, my psychiatrist, an autism advocacy group, and my career counselors who I met with every week. With their help and support, I've had some employment success and even got accepted into graduate school. I am grateful to this new network of support that has helped me start to move forward with my life.

Things are looking up now, though the process was slow and grueling at some points. The pain of missing these people who are very much alive but are now estranged to me necessitated grief, adjustment, and healing in order to move past the cold and lonely reality of what their absence left behind. However, by understanding the context in which these events took place, I am able to let go of that loneliness and make space for acceptance and, ultimately, forgiveness. Furthermore, through the cathartic process of writing about these difficult past events, I have allowed myself to put them to rest and free up energy for the present. Indeed, despite the grief I went through after some of the hardest times in my life last year, I now can focus on all the possibilities ahead of me. That is why I will continue to seek out the people and resources I need in order to not only survive, but thrive.

---

*Lee is a late 20s homebody from the US. They are a fan of Netflix, naps, and dogs of all kinds.*

# On Finding Yourself in Someone Else

*Noor Pervez (he/him/his)*

June 2013 marked the first of many times that I thought my life was over. I'd come to terms with the fact that I, a south Asian then-teenage girl, liked women, albeit in such a way that I felt extremely uncomfortable. My family thought of me as a sort of incredibly awkward duckling. I couldn't do much right. I wasn't popular with boys, and I had few friends. It felt as if I was being constricted in the double bind of expectations I faced in the transition years—grow up, and acknowledge who I actually was, and conform to the pristine young desi woman and future wife I was expected to be. Nothing about me felt right, and I felt that I was at a dead end. Then, I met Adam.

Adam was the first openly queer and autistic person I'd ever known. They held themselves with a casual confidence that I couldn't fathom. They were a friend's sister's partner, foisted at me when I finally came out a few months before my graduation.

"Here," Lindsey said, "a bisexual is like a lesbian. Maybe they can help you feel better." I didn't know how to wrap my head around that, but I also couldn't argue. Was that what I was? Lesbian? Something about the word felt foreign, but I swallowed it down. We texted about policy and legislation facing LGBT people and realized immediately that we were both policy-heads.

I clicked with Adam in a way that I didn't with many others. We went into student organization leadership with equal vigor, and I found myself making friends with a huge number of people in the group. Soon, it was as though I was injected with life. I walked through campus with my head down, but when I entered Rainbow Guard on Friday, I flourished. I bounced on the heels of my feet, rolled and shook and said hello to every single new person. I was like a puppy seeing the world for the first time—everything felt new and immediately like home at the same time. It felt as if this was all I'd ever been meant to be, and just never knew it.

I soon realized, through gentle prodding and help from a therapist and my first boyfriend, that I was trans and autistic. The words were like entry into the room all over again—like tumbling, bouncing, screaming joy. It felt as if every part of me made sense in a way that it never had before. I started dressing in ways that felt affirming to me—bright colors, stimmy fabrics, things that jangled when I walked. Thinking back to my childhood, I remembered not having traditional speech. I remembered speaking the way that I did in group, repeating, playing with words like toys, smashing random ones together and sometimes just making sounds. I remembered the repeated insistence that I look "pretty" for other people, the screaming when my mother pulled a too-thin brush through my hair. I remembered my hands being shoved down, being told that my voice was inconvenient and impolite, a target on my back that read "problem child" or "special ed," with the intent of separating me.

When I think of that time, of growing up in a family that was trying to prepare me for a world that saw me as a terror threat as I aged, I understand that a lot of the silencing behavior came from a place of trying to protect me. I also recognize it as traumatic. Holding both in my hands is incredibly hard. I fluctuate between blaming my family for hurting me so intensely and seeing the restraint in their faces, the way they guard their words when they speak, playing respectability politics to try to keep a roof over their heads and food in their mouths.

What I wish, more than anything, is that I'd had the freedom to be who I am earlier. I wish I was able to try different pronoun sets as a child. I wish that I could have worn whatever made me feel happy, whether that was colorful makeup, or certain fabrics, or baggy pants. In my dreams, when I see young Noor, I see an autistic child who had access to that label without the threat of applied behavior analysis or separation from my friends hanging over me. Jangling bracelets, bhangra practice, access to the outside world and all of its beauty without the harsh edges—I believe in the infinity of possibilities that I should have had, and I believe that our kids can have it. It will come.

---

*Noor is a community organizer who strongly believes that the future will be better if we work together across identities.*

# Meetings and Partings

*Heather Rowan Nichol (they/them/their)*

The journey of life is meetings and partings,

As we part from the womb,
and rejoin at the breast.
Early years, many meetings,
Our parents' friendships
Slowly, we make our own,
With luck the ties of blood a source of strength,
Not a source of hardship.

Now, deeper meetings,
Close friends of our choosing
our own patterns of life.
Will I be laughed at, misjudged?
Will they think me a creep?
And could it be possible,
Acceptance, Caring, Sharing.
And how will this be—
Ministry to many,
or life with one special.

And we meet
And part
And learn.

May our meetings be hopeful
And our partings be with love.

With the passage of time we learn,
To follow the promptings of love and truth in our hearts,
Not the fears or the ought to's of others
Nor the fear and guilt in ourselves.
With the passing of fear "I love"
No more means "I need you"
"I love" means "I rejoice at your existence on Earth"

And the wrong we do dies with us
And the love we leave lives on with us
Even as our bodies rejoin the Earth,
When we have moved to freer living.

---

*Heather Rowan Nichol is a 55-year-old electrical and electronic engineer, with both a day job and a small business. Their favorite pastime is traveling alone by bicycle.*

# Endnotes

1   Transgender is a word that describes a person who does not identify with the gender they were assigned at birth, typically based on what genitalia they were born with.

2   Gender assigned at birth is a phrase used to describe the phenomenon of looking at an infant's genitalia and announcing "it's a girl" or "it's a boy," depending on what those genitalia look like.

3   For many years, three Autistic boys were diagnosed for every one Autistic girl diagnosed. Newer theories posit a diagnostic bias and/or parental reporting bias rather than an actual gender skew. For reference, see Supekar, K., and Menon, V. (2015) "Sex differences in structural organization of motor systems and their dissociable links with repetitive/restricted behaviors in children with autism." *Molecular Autism*, 6(4), 50. doi:10.1186/s13229-015-0042-z. And Holtmann, M., *et al.* (2007) "Autism spectrum disorders: Sex differences in autistic behaviour domains and coexisting psychopathology." *Developmental Medicine & Child Neurology*, 49(5), 361–366. doi:10.1111/j.1469-8749.2007.00361.x.

4   Ehrensaft, D. (2018) "Double helix rainbow kids." *Journal of Autism and Developmental Disorders*, 48(12), 4079–4081. doi: 10.1007/s10803-018-3716-5.

5   "Data & Statistics on Autism Spectrum Disorder." Centers for Disease Control and Prevention. Retrieved from www.cdc.gov/ncbddd/autism/data.html.

6   "Autism Facts and History." National Autistic Society. Retrieved from www.autism.org.uk/about/what-is/myths-facts-stats.aspx.

7   Non-binary genders are any gender that is not strictly 100 percent male or 100 percent female. There are an infinite variety of non-binary genders.

8   Cisgender is a word that describes a person who identifies with the gender they were assigned at birth.

9   Binary genders are the "classic" two genders: 100 percent male or 100 percent female. Both Trans people and cis people (and those who identify outside those two categories) can have binary genders. In other words, a gender does not have to be assigned at birth to be a binary gender.

10  American Psychiatric Association (2017) *Diagnostic and Statistical Manual of Mental Disorders: DSM-5.* Washington DC: American Psychiatric Association.

11  Veale, J.F. (2008) "Prevalence of transsexualism among New Zealand passport holders." *Australian and New Zealand Journal of Psychiatry*, 42(10), 887–889. doi: 10.1080/00048670802345490.

12  Collin, L., Reisner, S.L., Tangpricha, V., & Goodman, M. (2016) "Prevalence of transgender depends on the 'case' definition: A systematic review." *The Journal of Sexual Medicine*, 13(4), 613–626. doi: 10.1016/j.jsxm.2016.02.001.

13  Nobili, A., Glazebrook, C., Bouman, W.P., Glidden, D., *et al.* (2018) "Autistic traits in treatment-seeking transgender adults." *Journal of Autism and Developmental Disorders*, 48(12), 3984–3994. doi: 10.1007/s10803-018-3557-2.

14  Shumer, D.E., Reisner, S.L., Edwards-Leeper, L., & Tishelman, A. (2016) "Evaluation of Asperger syndrome in youth presenting to a gender dysphoria clinic." *LGBT Health*, 3(5), 387–390. doi: 10.1089/lgbt.2015.0070.

15  Becerra-Culqui, T.A., Liu, Y., Nash, R., Cromwell, L., *et al.* (2018) "Mental health of transgender and gender nonconforming youth compared with their peers." *Pediatrics*, 141(5). doi: 10.1542/peds.2017-3845.

16  Dragon, C.N., Guerino, P., Ewald, E., & Laffan, A.M. (2017) "Transgender medicare beneficiaries and chronic conditions: Exploring fee-for-service claims data." *LGBT Health*, 4(6), 404–411. doi: 10.1089/lgbt.2016.0208.

17  Cheung, A.S., Ooi, O., Leemaqz, S., Cundill, P., *et al.* (2018) "Sociodemographic and clinical characteristics of transgender adults in Australia." *Transgender Health*, 3(1), 229–238. doi: 10.1089/trgh.2018.0019.

18  Pasterski, V., Gilligan, L., & Curtis, R. (2013) "Traits of autism spectrum disorders in adults with gender dysphoria." *Archives of Sexual Behavior*, 43(2), 387–393. doi: 10.1007/s10508-013-0154-5.

19  Nahata, L., Quinn, G.P., Caltabellotta, N.M., & Tishelman, A.C. (2017) "Mental health concerns and insurance denials among transgender adolescents." *LGBT Health*, 4(3), 188–193. doi: 10.1089/lgbt.2016.0151.

20  De Vries, A.L.C.D., Noens, I.L.J., Cohen-Kettenis, P.T., Berckelaer-Onnes, I.A.V., & Doreleijers, T.A. (2010) "Autism spectrum disorders in gender dysphoric children and adolescents." *Journal of Autism and Developmental Disorders*, 40(8), 930–936. doi: 10.1007/s10803-010-0935-9.

21  Stagg, S.D. & Vincent, J. (2019) "Autistic traits in individuals self-defining as transgender or nonbinary." *European Psychiatry*, 61, 17–22. doi: 10.1016/j.eurpsy.2019.06.003.

22  Van Der Miesen, A.I.V.D., Hurley, H., & Vries, A.L.D. (2016) "Gender dysphoria and autism spectrum disorder: A narrative review." *International Review of Psychiatry*, 28(1), 70–80. doi: 10.3109/09540261.2015.1111199.

23  Hisle-Gorman, E., Landis, C.A., Susi, A., Schvey, N.A., *et al.* (2019) "Gender dysphoria in children with autism spectrum disorder." *LGBT Health*, 6(3), 95–100. doi: 10.1089/lgbt.2018.0252.

24  George, R. & Stokes, M.A. (2017). "Gender identity and sexual orientation in autism spectrum disorder." *Autism*, 22(8), 970–982. doi: 10.1177/1362361317714587.

25  Van Der Miesen, A.I.V.D., Hurley, H., & Vries, A.L.D. (2016) "Gender dysphoria and autism spectrum disorder: A narrative review." *International Review of Psychiatry,* 28(1), 70–80. doi: 10.3109/09540261.2015.1111199.

26  George, R. & Stokes, M.A. (2017) "Gender identity and sexual orientation in autism spectrum disorder." *Autism,* 22(8), 970–982. doi: 10.1177/1362361317714581.

27  Strang, J.F., Kenworthy, L., Dominska, A., Sokoloff, J., *et al.* (2014) "Increased gender variance in autism spectrum disorders and attention deficit hyperactivity disorder." *Archives of Sexual Behavior,* 43(8), 1525–1533. doi: 10.1007/s10508-014-0285-3.

28  Van Der Miesen, A.I.V.D., Hurley, H., & Vries, A.L.D. (2016) "Gender dysphoria and autism spectrum disorder: A narrative review." *International Review of Psychiatry,* 28(1), 70–80. doi: 10.3109/09540261.2015.1111199.

29  Dewinter, J., Graaf, H.D., & Begeer, S. (2017) "Sexual orientation, gender identity, and romantic relationships in adolescents and adults with autism spectrum disorder." *Journal of Autism and Developmental Disorders,* 47(9), 2927–2934. doi: 10.1007/s10803-017-3199-9.

30  Van Der Miesen, A.I.V.D., Hurley, H., & Vries, A.L.D. (2016) "Gender dysphoria and autism spectrum disorder: A narrative review." *International Review of Psychiatry,* 28(1), 70–80. doi: 10.3109/09540261.2015.1111199.

31  Dewinter, J., Graaf, H.D., & Begeer, S. (2017) "Sexual orientation, gender identity, and romantic relationships in adolescents and adults with autism spectrum disorder." *Journal of Autism and Developmental Disorders,* 47(9), 2927–2934. doi: 10.1007/s10803-017-3199-9.

32  Cassidy, S. & Rodgers, J. (2017) "Understanding and prevention of suicide in autism." *The Lancet,* 4(6), 11. doi: 10.1016/S2215-0366(17)30162-1.

33  Moody, C. & Grant Smith, N. "Suicide protective factors among trans adults." *Archives of Sexual Behavior,* Springer US, July 2013. Retrieved from www.ncbi.nlm.nih.gov/pmc/articles/PMC3722435.

34  Jones, S.R. (2016) "Autism and homelessness: The real crisis." *Rooted in Rights,* 18 October, 2016. Retrieved from https://rootedinrights.org/autism-and-homelessness-the-real-crisis.

35  "Housing & Homelessness." National Center for Transgender Equality. Retrieved from https://transequality.org/issues/housing-homelessness.

36  Calleja, S., *et al.* (2019) "The disparities of healthcare access for adults with autism spectrum disorder." *Medicine,* 98(7). doi:10.1097/md.0000000000014480.

37  Safer, J.D., *et al.* (2016) "Barriers to health care for transgender individuals." *Current Opinion in Endocrinology & Diabetes and Obesity,* 23(2), 168–171. doi:10.1097/MED.0000000000000227.

38  Ratcliffe, K. (1999) "Rhetorical listening: A trope for interpretive invention and a 'Code of Cross-Cultural Conduct.'" *College Composition and Communication,* 51(2), 195–224. doi:10.2307/359039, p.46.

39  Heilker, P. & Yergeau, M. (2011) "Autism as a rhetoric." *College English,* 73(5), 485–497. JSTOR, www.jstor.org/stable/23052337.

40 Yergeau, M. (2018) *Authoring Autism: On Rhetoric and Neurological Queerness*. Durham, NC: Duke University Press.

41 Barthes, R. (1992) "Myth Today." In C. Harrison and P. Wood (eds), *Art in Theory* (pp.687–693). London: Blackwell.

42 Menosky, J. & Moore, R.D. (1991) "In Theory." *Star Trek: The Next Generation*. Dir. Patrick Stewart. Syndicated. 3 June 1991. Television.

43 Butler, J. (1990) *Gender Trouble: Feminism and the Subversion of Identity*. New York, NY: Routledge.

44 Heilker, P. & Yergeau, M. (2011) "Autism as a rhetoric." *College English*, 73(5), 485–497. JSTOR, www.jstor.org/stable/23052337, p.491.

45 Keegan, C.M. (2013) "Moving bodies: Sympathetic migrations in transgender narrativity." *Genders 1998-2013*, University of Colorado Boulder, 1 June 2013. Retrieved from www.colorado.edu/gendersarchive1998-2013/2013/06/01/moving-bodies-sympathetic-migrations-transgender-narrativity.

46 Echevarria, R. (1995) "Facets." *Star Trek: Deep Space Nine*. Dir. Cliff Bole. Syndicated. 12 June. 1995. Television.

47 Stryker, S. (2000) "Transsexuality: The Postmodern Body and/as Technology." In D. Bell & B. Kennedy (eds), *The Cybercultures Reader* (pp.38–50). New York, NY: Routledge, p.592.

48 Menosky, J. & Dial, B. (1994) "The Alternate." *Star Trek: Deep Space Nine*. Dir. David Carson. Syndicated. 9 Jan. 1994. Television.

49 Butler, J. (1999) *Gender Trouble: Feminism and the Subversion of Identity* (2nd ed.). Abingdon: Routledge.

50 Hillary, A. (2014) "The Erasure of Queer Autistic People." In C. Wood (ed.) *Criptiques* (pp.121–145). San Bernardino, CA: May Day, p.121.

51 Egner, J.E. (2018) "'The disability rights community was never mine:' Neuroqueer disidentification." *Gender & Society*. 33(1), 123–147.

52 Montgomery, C. (2012/2001) "Critic of the Dawn." In J. Bascom (ed.), *Loud Hands: Autistic People Speaking* (pp.71–87). Washington DC: The Autistic Press, p.79.

53 Hillary, A. (2018) "Am I Confused? Are You?" In M.E. Brown & D. Burill (eds), *Challenging Genders: Non-Binary Experiences of Those Assigned Female at Birth* (pp.77–82). Miami, FL: Boundless Endeavors.

54 Hillary, A. (2014) "The Erasure of Queer Autistic People." In C. Wood (ed.), *Criptiques* (pp.121–145). San Bernardino, CA: May Day.

55 ibid, p.121.

56 Duane, D. (1983–present). *Young Wizards* (series). Various Publishers.

57 Kourti, M. & MacLeod, A. (2018) "'I Don't Feel Like a Gender, I Feel Like Myself': Autistic Individuals Raised as Girls Exploring Gender Identity." *Autism in Adulthood: Knowledge, Practice, and Policy*. Retrieved from https://doi.org/10.1089/aut.2018.0001.

58 Lawson, W. (2005) *Sex, Sexuality and the Autism Spectrum*. London and Philadelphia, PA: Jessica Kingsley Publishers.

59 ibid, p.143.

**60** Lawson, W.B. & Lawson, B.M. (2017) *Transitioning Together: One Couple's Journey of Gender and Identity Discovery*. London and Philadelphia, PA: Jessica Kingsley Publishers.

**61** Possibly forever.

**62** I hope the notes will give you a taste of the food and architecture, without requiring you to fully learn the language of land inside my skull.

**63** Really terrible. Like food that had been pre-digested or something. I remember that I couldn't bring myself to look at it, but I also have a very clear memory that it looked like puke on Wonder Bread. I'm pretty sure I made up that mental image, and that I really did never bring myself to look.

**64** With frosted and leaded glass instead of the clear glass of the other doors.

**65** Why do they always turn off the lights and cover the windows in ASD classrooms? When my son was going to be put in one, I'm sure the darkness was part of what really shut him down. Sitting by an open window is one of the accommodations he often requests.

**66** If you want this in my authentic voice, you must watch *Rita*, until you get to the part where Hjørdis comments on Rita's "many many men." Listen to the Danish words "Mange Mange menn..." there it is. Now use a good, strong male voice actor and Hjørdis' inflexion. Got it? Good. "Hjørdis and Rita on the school steps" can now cover this meaning.

**67** We did not get along well in those early days, the internet and I, because the internet was too slow and would never catch on, but bulletin board systems were "the bomb" because I could play *Star Trek* role-playing games (rpgs) on them—but these are details you do not really need to know right now.

**68** I did not categorize it as "boys" at the time. It was a category of people that includes memories of boys in advertisements, my father, kids at day care, and one particular uncle who I somehow tagged as extra-masculine well into my teens. I still have this category in my mind, and though I am aware of it having undergone some change, there is a hard core to it that convinces me that there is *something* essential about gender.

**69** Lewin, E. (2009) *Gay Fatherhood: Narratives of Family and Citizenship in America*. Chicago: University of Chicago Press, p.161.

**70** Woolf, V. (1929) *A Room of One's Own*. New York: Harcourt, Brace and Company, p.192.